MY FIRST

## My First Encyclopedia of

# WHY ?

# CONTENTS

## 🦋 The countryside

Why do trees lose their **leaves** in autumn?, 6
Why do we need **earth worms**?, 7
Why is **grass** green?, 7
Why do plants and **trees** have roots?, 7
Why shouldn't we touch **mushrooms**?, 8
Why do **woodpeckers** drum on trees with their beaks?, 9
Why do **squirrels** collect nuts and hide them?, 9
Why do **pine cones** open and close?, 9
Why do **caterpillars** turn into butterflies?, 10
Why do we blow on **dandelion** heads?, 11
Why do **nettles** sting?, 11
Why do people kiss under the **mistletoe**?, 11
Why do **spiders** weave webs?, 12
Why do **mosquitoes** bite?, 12
Why do **tadpoles** turn into frogs?, 12
Why do we put out food for the **birds** in winter?, 13
Why do birds build **nests**?, 13
Why do **bees** make honey?, 13
Why do we cry when we chop **onions**?, 14
Why do we say a **tomato** is a fruit?, 14
Why do **carrots** grow underground?, 14
Why do **flowers** turn into fruit?, 15
Why do **cherries** have stones?, 15
Why do **maple tree seeds** spin round and round as they fall?, 15

## 🐟 The sea

Why is the water in the sea **salty**?, 16
Why does the **sea** rise up the beach and then go down again?, 16
Why are there **waves**?, 17
Why is the beach **sandy**?, 17
Why does the **hermit crab** keep changing its shell?, 18
Why does **seaweed** have little bubbles on it that pop?, 18
Why do **starfish** have five arms?, 18
Why do **crabs** walk sideways?, 19
Why are there **little holes** and **piles of sand** all over the beach?, 19
Why do **fish** have holes on either side of their head?, 20

Why do **sharks** have so many teeth?, 21
Why do **jellyfish** sting?, 21
Why do **flatfish** have both eyes on one side of their head?, 21
Why does the **pufferfish** blow itself up like a balloon?, 21
Why do **sperm whales** have so many scars?, 22
Why do **dolphins** come to the surface of the water to breathe?, 22
Why do **whales** have blowholes?, 23
Why do **seabirds** dive-bomb into the sea?, 23
Why do **boats** float?, 24
Why do **submarines** go underwater?, 25
Why are there so many **fishing knots**?, 25
Why do fishermen catch **fish**?, 25
Why are goods transported by **ship**?, 25

# The mountains

Why are there hardly any **trees** at the top of mountains?, 26
Why are mountain **peaks** covered in **snow** in summer?, 26
Why does it get **colder** as you climb higher up a mountain?, 27
Why do **climbers** wear masks at high altitudes?, 27
Why are **mountain streams** so full in the spring?, 28
Why are there so many **pine trees** in the mountains?, 28
Why are there **mountains**?, 28
Why do some mountains have **strange shapes**?, 29
Why do **volcanoes** form mountains?, 29
Why do **eagles** circle round and round in the sky?, 30
Why do **marmots** whistle when you get close?, 30
Why do **bears** fish in streams?, 30
Why do some animals turn **white** in winter?, 30
Why are there **wolves** in some mountains?, 31
Why do people **herd** animals up into the mountains for the summer?, 31
Why do some **animals** prefer to live in the mountains?, 31
Why are the **wild flowers** so brightly coloured in the mountains?, 32
Why does it **snow**?, 33
Why do we slide on **snow**?, 33
Why are no two **snowflakes** ever the same?, 33
Why do **crevasses** form in glaciers?, 34
Why are there **avalanches** in the mountains?, 34
Why do people choose to **live** in mountains?, 35
Why do people build **dams**?, 35
Why do people dig **tunnels**?, 35

## 🦘 Animals

Why are there so many **different** animals?, 36
Why do animals often come together where there is **water**?, 36
Why do some animals **eat** other animals?, 37
Why do some animals prefer to come out **at night**?, 37
Why do **elephants** hold each other's tails?, 38
Why do we say the **lion** is the king of the animals?, 38
Why do **zebras** have stripes?, 38
Why do **giraffes** have such long necks?, 38
Why do **parrots** copy what you say?, 39
Why do **dromedaries** have humps?, 40
Why do **tortoises** move so slowly?, 40
Why don't **snakes** have legs?, 40
Why do animals hide **underground** in the desert?, 40
Why are **polar bears** white?, 41
Why do **reindeer** have antlers?, 41
Why do baby **penguins** perch on their parents' feet?, 41
Why do **chicks** come from eggs?, 42
Why does a **rabbit's** nose keep twitching?, 42
Why do **cows** produce milk?, 42
Why do **swallows** return every year in the spring?, 43
Why do **cats** always fall on their feet?, 43
Why does a **dog** wag its tail?, 43
Why did **dinosaurs** disappear?, 44
Why are **flamingoes** pink?, 44
Why are there so few **pandas**?, 44
Why do **bats** sleep upside down?, 45
Why do **chameleons** change colour?, 45
Why do mother **kangaroos** have pouches?, 45

## 👶 Our body

Why do we each have a **name**?, 46
Why do children **grow**?, 46
Why are there **boys** and **girls**?, 47
Why are we each **different**?, 47
Why do we have a **head**, a **torso**, **arms** and **legs**?, 48
Why do we have **bones**?, 49
Why do we have **thoughts** in our heads?, 49

Why is our body covered in **skin**?, 49
Why do we have **muscles**?, 49
Why can't we eat just one sort of **food**?, 50
Why do we **pee** and **poo**?, 50
Why do we lose our **teeth**?, 50
Why do we **breathe**?, 51
Why do we **sleep**?, 51
Why does our **heart** beat?, 51
Why do we have **five senses**?, 52
Why do we **dream**?, 53
Why do we **laugh**?, 53
Why do we **cry**?, 53
Why do babies spend such a **long** time in their **mother's tummies**?, 54
Why do we have **tummy buttons**?, 54
Why do mummies have **babies**?, 54
Why do we **look like** our parents?, 55
Why can't babies **walk**?, 55

Why is the Earth **round**?, 58
Why do we have **seasons**?, 59
Why is it cold at the **poles**?, 60
Why does lava erupt from **volcanoes**?, 60
Why is there **sand** in the desert?, 60
Why are there **stalactites** and **stalagmites** in caves?, 61
Why is there **water** underground?, 61
Why did prehistoric people make **cave paintings**?, 61
Why are storms so **noisy**?, 62
Why are there **clouds**?, 62
Why does it **rain**?, 62
Why are there **rainbows**?, 63
Why does the **wind** blow?, 63
Why does the **Moon** change shape?, 64
Why do **stars** come out at night?, 64
Why do we see **shooting stars**?, 64
Why is the **Sun** hot?, 65
Why isn't there life on other **planets**?, 65

## ❓ Why quizz, 66

## 🌐 Earth and sky

Why are there **rivers**?, 56
Why are we able to live on **Earth**?, 56
Why are there underground **caves**?, 57
Why is the **sky** blue?, 57
Why do people call the Earth the **blue planet**?, 58
Why don't we **fall off** the Earth?, 58
Why do we have **day and night**?, 58

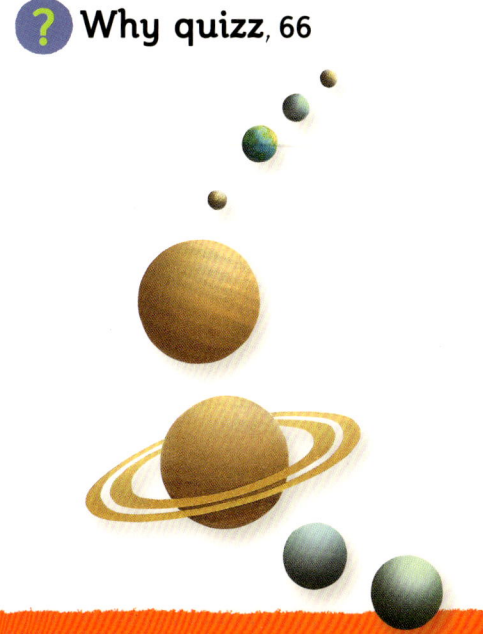

# The countryside

Trees, plants and animals exist together in the countryside. The way they each live and grow changes at different times of the day and night, and at different times of the year. Here are some of their secrets.

## Why do we need **earthworms**?

Earthworms play an important role in nature. They burrow into the ground and throw up soft, digested soil. The holes they make let air and water into the soil. This helps plants to grow.

## Why do trees lose their **leaves** in autumn?

The trees are slowing down in preparation for winter. They shed their dead leaves and conserve energy during the cold months.

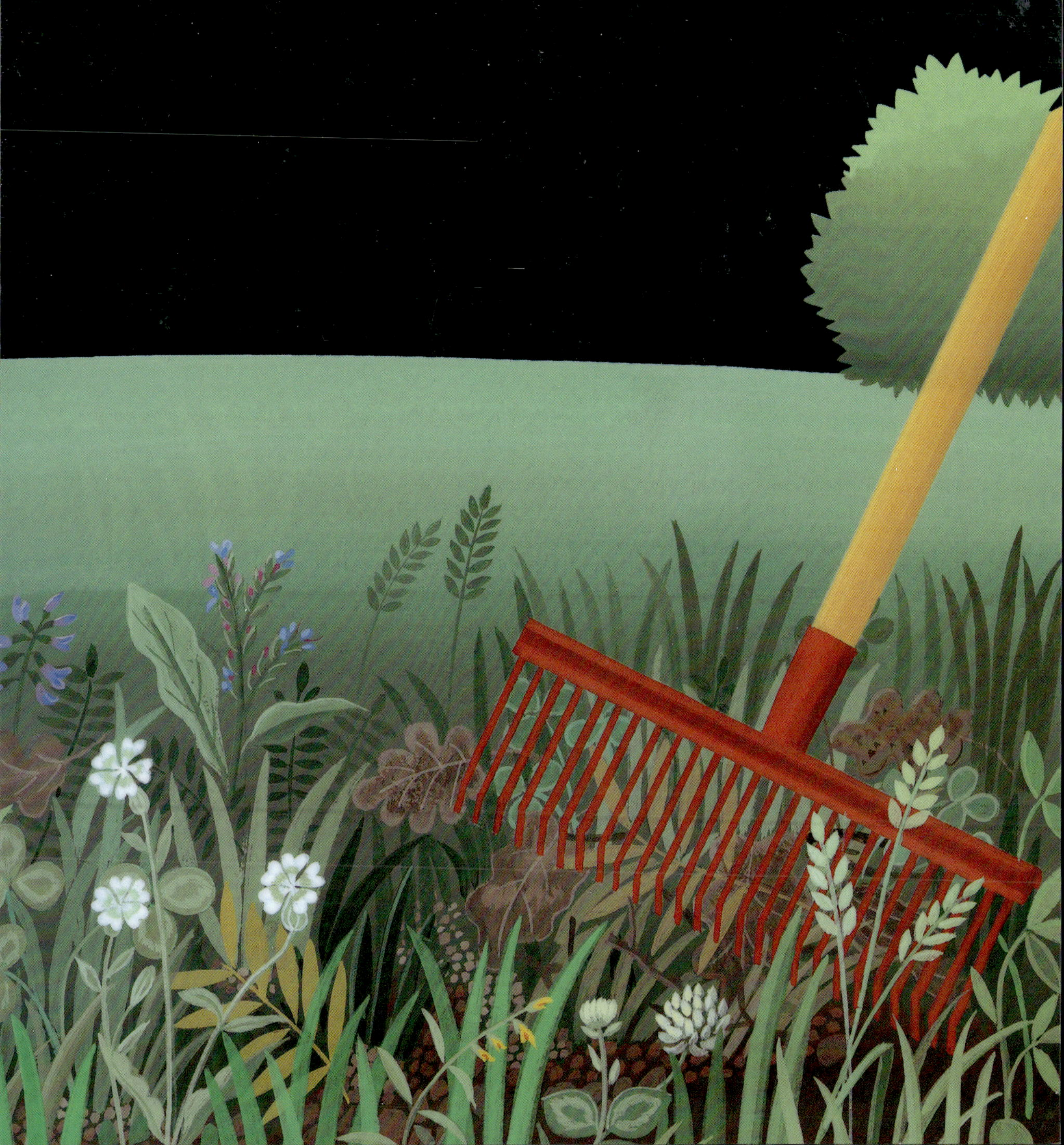

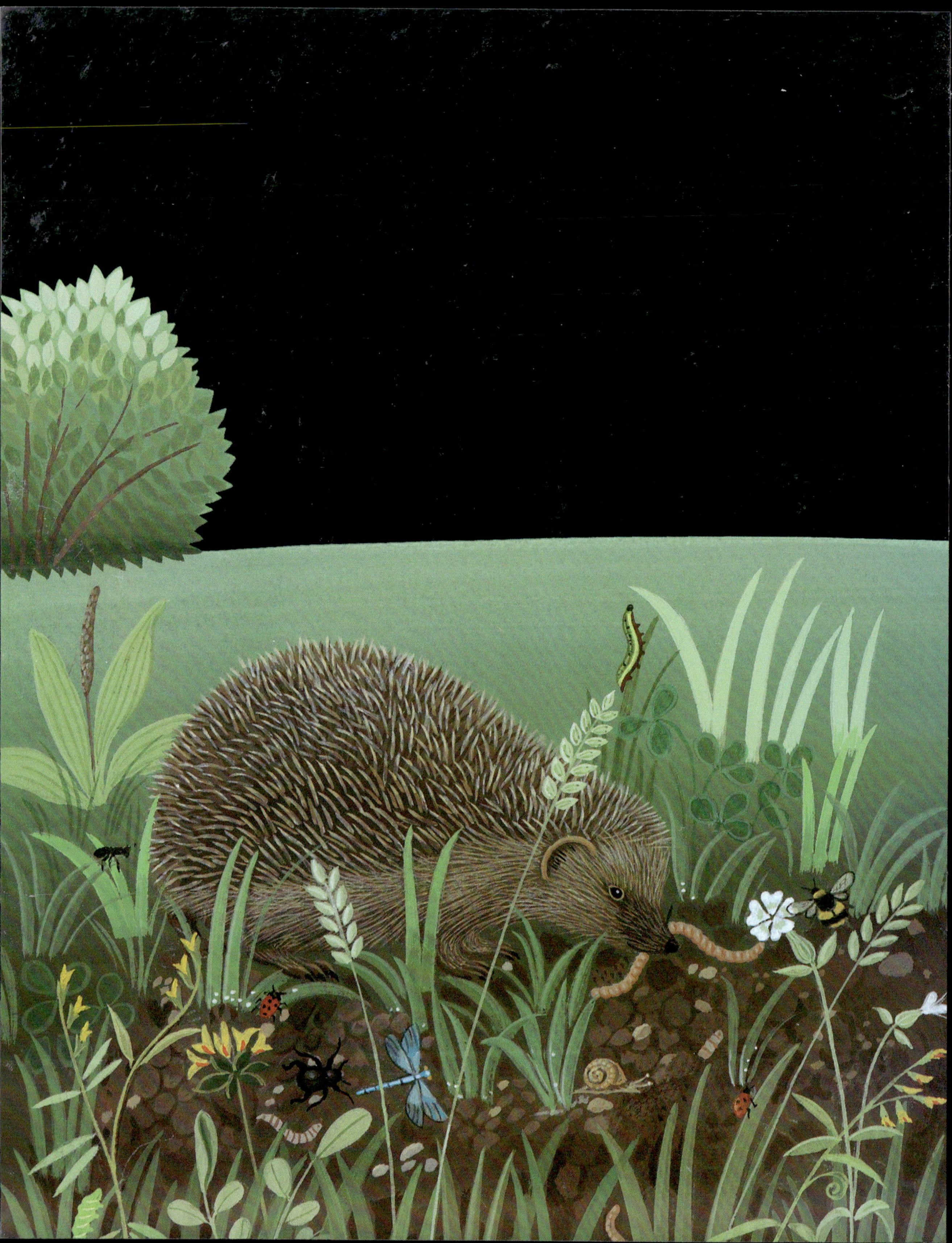

## Why is grass green?

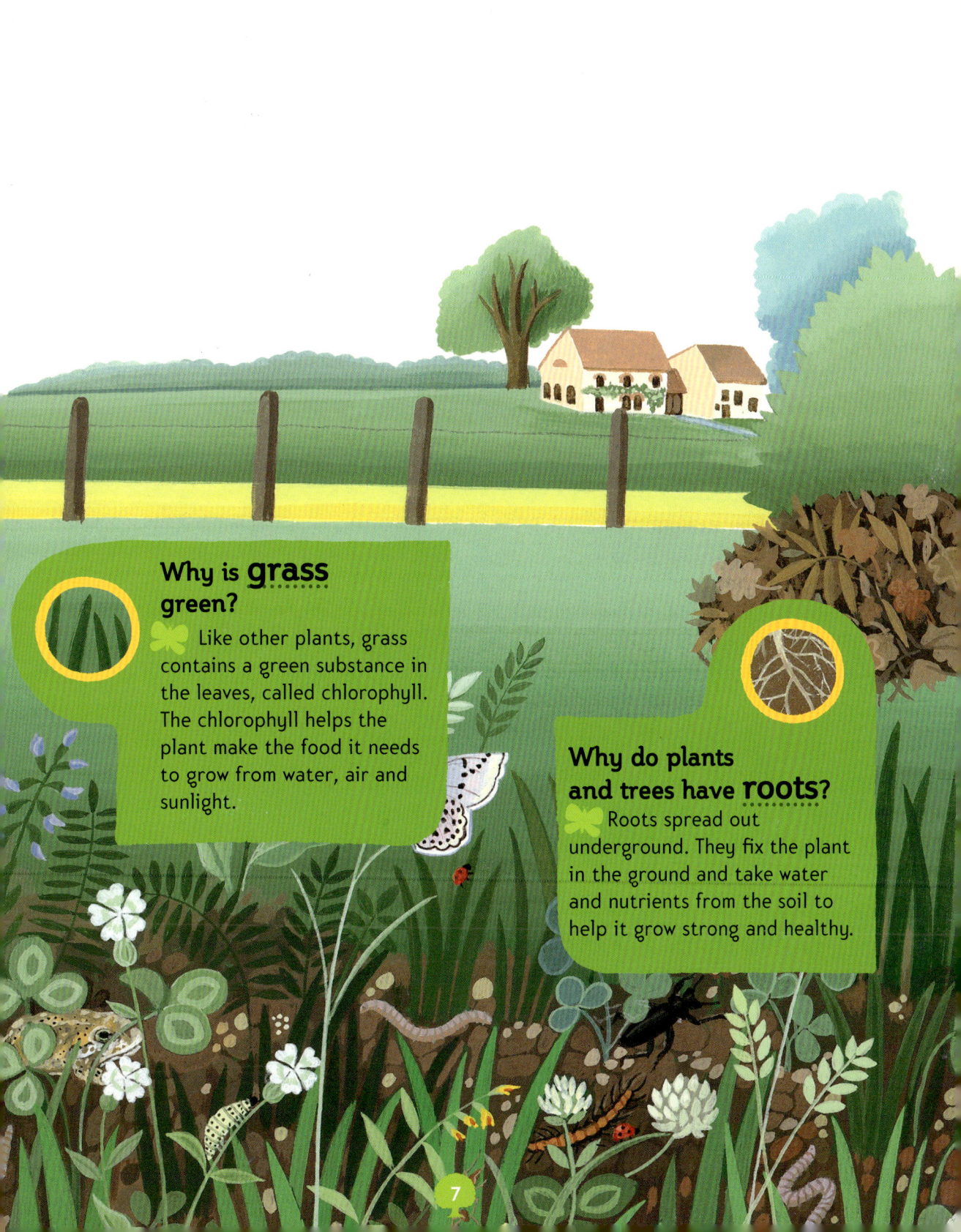

Like other plants, grass contains a green substance in the leaves, called chlorophyll. The chlorophyll helps the plant make the food it needs to grow from water, air and sunlight.

## Why do plants and trees have roots?

Roots spread out underground. They fix the plant in the ground and take water and nutrients from the soil to help it grow strong and healthy.

# Why shouldn't we touch mushrooms?

Some mushrooms are poisonous and can make us ill if we eat them. It is very difficult to know which ones they are. So it is better not to touch them.

Russula

Horn of plenty

Field mushroom

Chanterelle

Horsehair toadstool

Caesar's mushroom

Bolete

Shaggy ink cap

Ring

Stem

Gills

Morel

Volva

## Poisonous Mushrooms

Fly agaric

Death cap

Fairy ring mushroom

Cortinarius

Destroying angel

Devil's bolete

Lepiota helveola

Funeral bell

## Why do **woodpeckers** drum on trees with their beaks?

🦋 Woodpeckers don't sing. They mark their territory and attract a mate by drumming loudly on a tree trunk. This also makes the grubs inside the tree trunk easier to catch.

## Why do **squirrels** collect nuts and hide them?

🦋 Squirrels need to store up enough food during the warmer months to last them through winter when food is hard to find. As summer ends they start collecting nuts and hiding them away in secret places.

## Why do **pine cones** open and close?

🦋 Pine cones open when it's dry, and close when it's wet. When it's warm and dry, they open and release the seeds inside them, which are called pine kernels.

Closed pine cone

Open pine cone

**Did you know?**
A squirrel's bushy tail acts like a parachute as it jumps from branch to branch.

# Why do caterpillars turn into **butterflies?**

🦋 Caterpillars are butterfly larvae, or baby butterflies. As they grow bigger, they build a chrysalis and turn into butterflies.

**1** A caterpillar stays a caterpillar for a period of between a month and two years, depending on the type of caterpillar.

**2** When the time is right, the caterpillar builds a chrysalis around itself to protect it while it changes.

**3** Once the change is complete, the chrysalis breaks open and out comes the butterfly.

**4** Each butterfly has its own distinctive colours and markings.

The bud appears in early spring.

The flower is bright yellow.

Then the flower wilts.

The fluffy round seed-head forms.

The seeds are blown far and wide. Some take root and grow into new plants.

## Why do we blow on dandelion heads?

To have fun because the seeds fly away easily.

## Why do nettles sting?

The stems and leaves of nettles are covered in fine silky hairs that contain an acid. When you touch them, they sting and make your skin itch. It's their way of defending themselves.

## Why do people kiss under the mistletoe?

The ancient Druids believed mistletoe had special properties to keep evil away. We still bring sprigs of it into our houses at Christmas and kiss under them to bring us luck.

## Why do spiders weave webs?

🦋 To trap their prey. When an insect gets caught in the web, it starts to struggle. The spider feels the web shaking. It injects its prey with poison and then eats it.

## Why do mosquitoes bite?

🦋 Only female mosquitoes bite. Human blood provides them with rich food, which they need to lay their eggs. One bite allows them to lay between 100 and 200 eggs!

## Why do tadpoles turn into frogs?

🦋 Tadpoles are frog larvae, or baby frogs. Frogs lay their eggs in the spring. A week later they have hatched into tiny tadpoles. It takes four months for them to grow into frogs.

**1** When they are born, the tadpoles look like fish. Then their back legs start to appear, and finally their two front legs.

**2** Frogs have very strong, extra-long back legs. These are like springs which allow the frog to take huge leaps, and to jump clean out of the water.

## Why do we put out food for the **birds** in winter?

Birds are often hungry in winter. Food is hard to find when the ground is frozen or covered in snow. They are more often hungry than cold in winter!

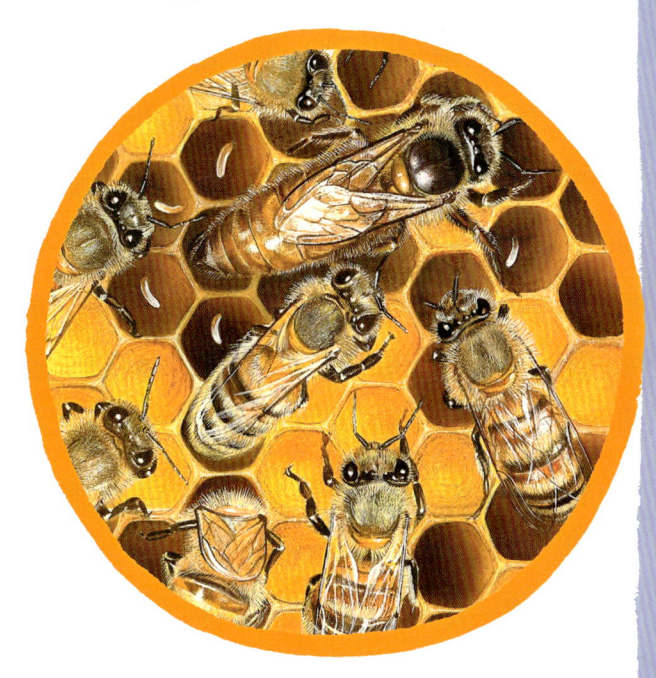

## Why do birds build **nests**?

Nests are safe places for birds to lay their eggs, and to sit on them. When the chicks hatch, they stay in the nest, out of danger, until they are ready to fly.

## Why do **bees** make honey?

Honey is their food. They feed off it in winter when there are no flowers from which to gather nectar. Their larvae also eat it until they are big enough to feed themselves.

**Did you know?** During the summer, worker bees only live for 40 days!

## Why do we cry when we chop **onions**?

Chopping an onion releases a sulphurous gas into the air that irritates our eyes. Our eyes water in order to rinse and protect themselves.

## Why do we say a **tomato** is a fruit?

Tomatoes grow in the same way as other fruits, from flowers. But in cooking, we say that all fruits are sweet and all vegetables savoury, so the tomato is what we call a vegetable-fruit!

## Why do **carrots** grow underground?

Carrots are roots. They belong to the root vegetable family, like turnips, radishes, and beetroot.

The carrot grows into a plant with a stem, leaves, flowers, seeds and a root, which we eat.

The carrot shoots grow

Carrot seeds

### Did you know?
People's favourite vegetable in many countries is the potato.

**1** There is pollen at the centre of the flower. Pollinators, like bees or the wind, carry the pollen from one flower to another.

**2** Once the flower has been pollinated, it withers. The fruit grows in its place, full of fresh seeds that will grow into new plants.

## Why do flowers turn into fruit?

🦋 To produce new plants. Inside the fruit are the seeds. Over time, these will grow into plants that will produce new flowers and fruit.

## Why do cherries have stones?

🦋 The cherry stones contain the seeds from which future cherry trees can grow. Most fruits contain seeds in the form of stones or pips, but bananas do not have either of these.

## Why do maple tree seeds spin round and round as they fall?

🦋 The seeds of the maple tree have wings called 'helicopters' that help them travel on the wind as they fall. In this way, they are more likely to land somewhere where the seeds can take root and grow.

# The sea

When you are on holiday, swimming and playing on the beach, do you ever wonder about the sea and the creatures that live in it? What makes the waves keep rolling in? Why is there so much sand? How do sea creatures live?

### Why is the water in the sea **salty**?

🐟 Because it has salt in it! Rain falling on the land over millions of years washes salt from the rocks. This water drains into rivers and out to sea, where the salt stays.

### Why does the sea **rise up** the beach and then **go down** again?

🐟 The Moon acts like a magnet on the water. When the Moon is over the sea, it pulls the water up towards it. This produces high tides. When the Moon moves away, the water moves back down, giving low tides.

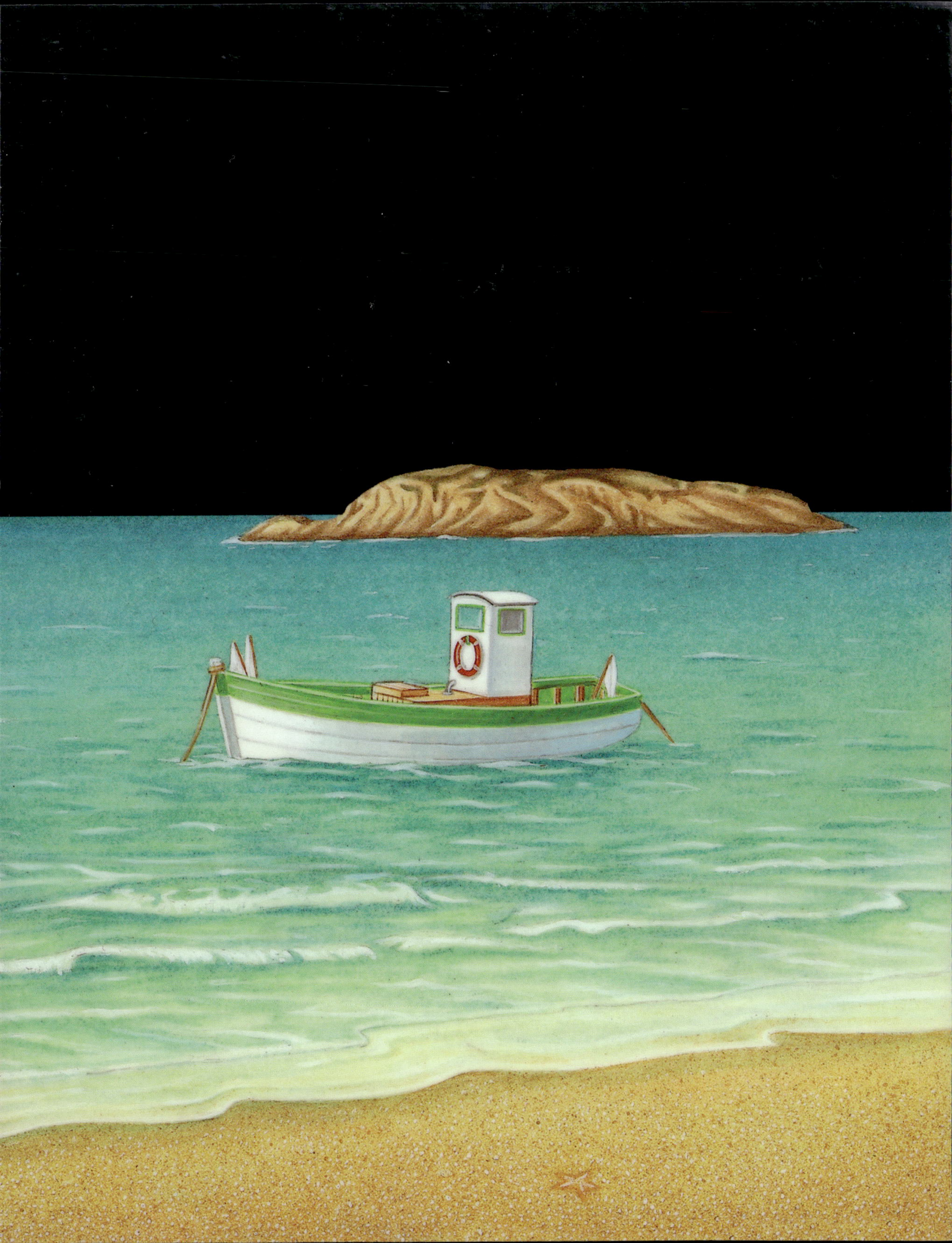

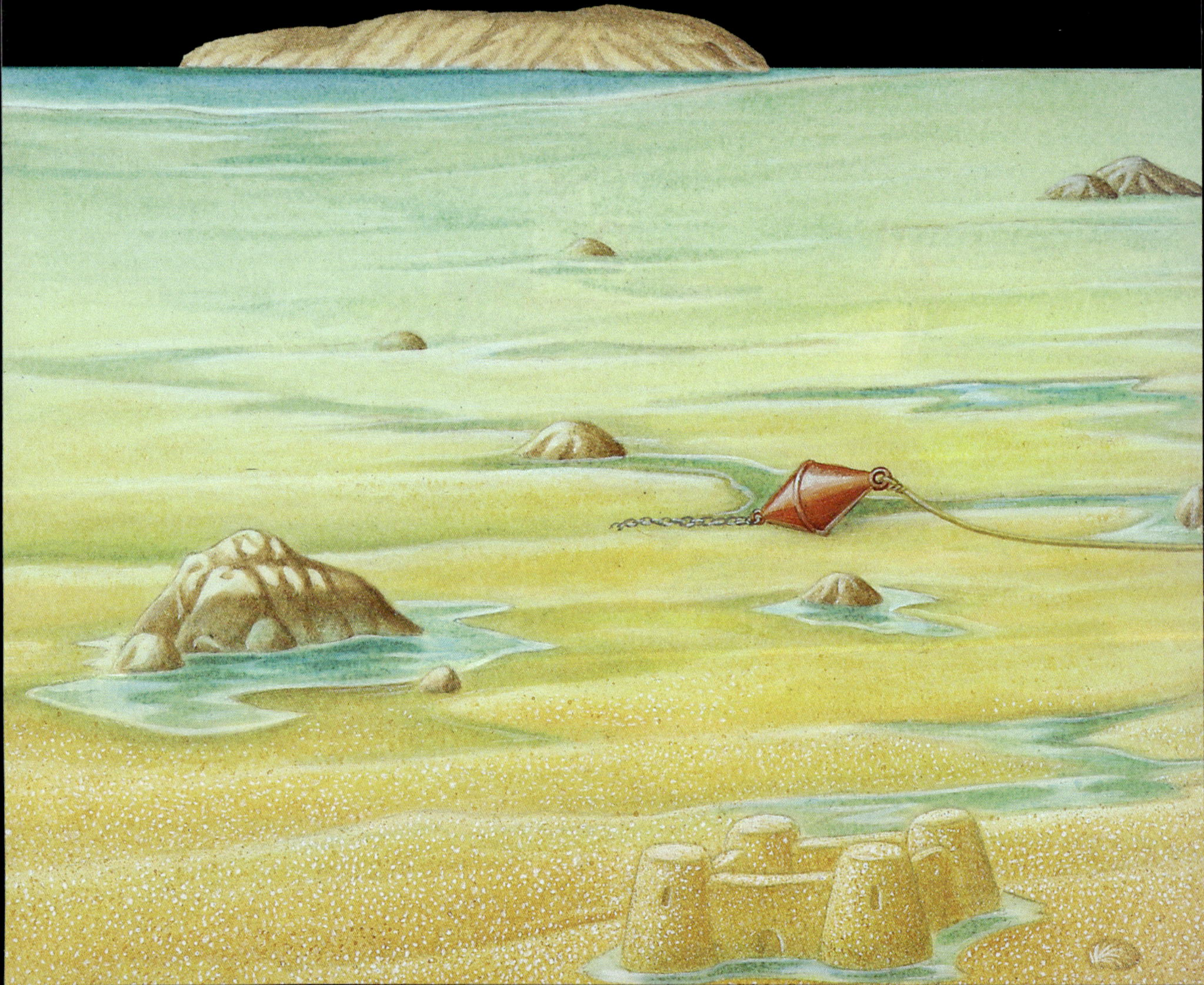

## Why are there waves?

🐟 Because of the wind. The wind blowing on the surface of the sea makes waves. The stronger the wind, the bigger the waves. Once they start, they continue across the water until they reach dry land.

## Why is the beach sandy?

🐟 The sand comes from rocks which are broken down by the sea over millions of years. Small stones and pebbles broken off from the rocks are slowly ground down by the sea until they become sand.

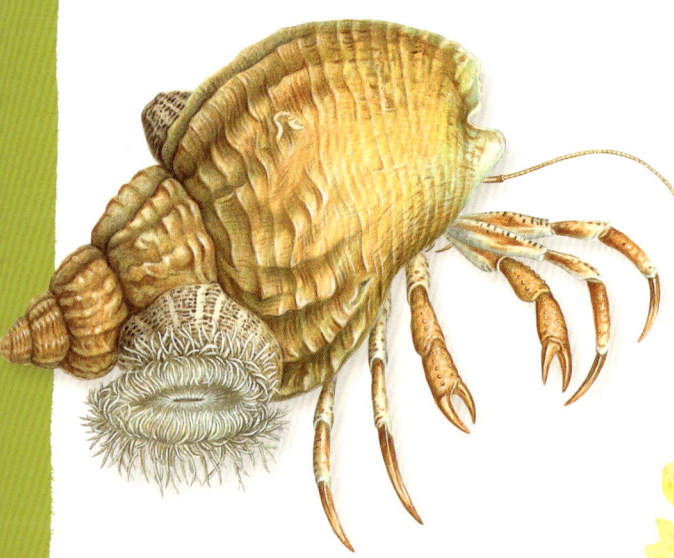

## Why does the hermit crab keep changing its shell?

The hermit crab has a soft fleshy body. To protect itself, it finds an empty seashell that it can fit into and carry around. When it gets too big for one shell it moves into a larger one.

## Why does seaweed have little bubbles on it that pop?

These are little pods, full of air. They allow the seaweed, which is attached to the seafloor, to float. The seaweed receives more light near the surface, which helps it grow and reproduce.

## Why do starfish have five arms?

The starfish's arms help it move around and feed. They are covered in suckers that make it easy to hold on to things. Some starfish have six arms, others even more.

## Why do crabs walk sideways?

Crabs have wide, flat shells. Their legs are on the sides of the shell and only bend sideways. This is good for digging in the sand, but means they can only move sideways, not forwards or backwards.

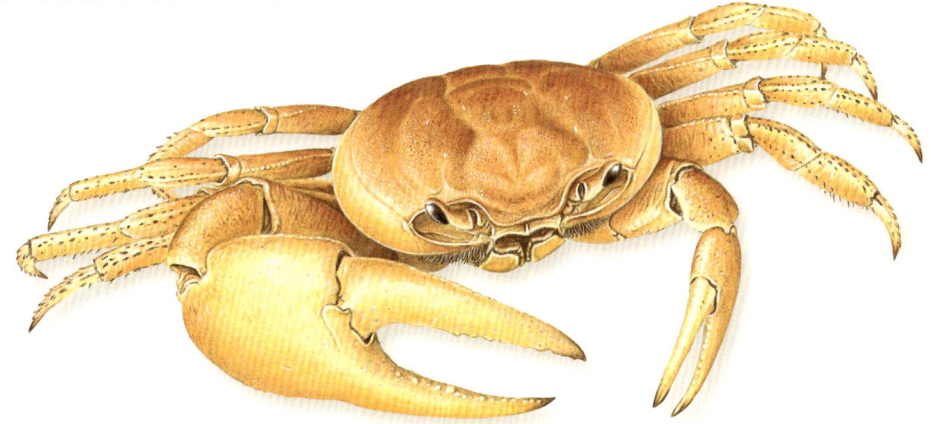

## Why are there little holes and piles of sand all over the beach?

In each little hole, a shellfish is hiding. The hole lets in air so it can breathe. Under each little pile of sand there is a worm. The little pile is the sand the worm throws up as it eats through the sand.

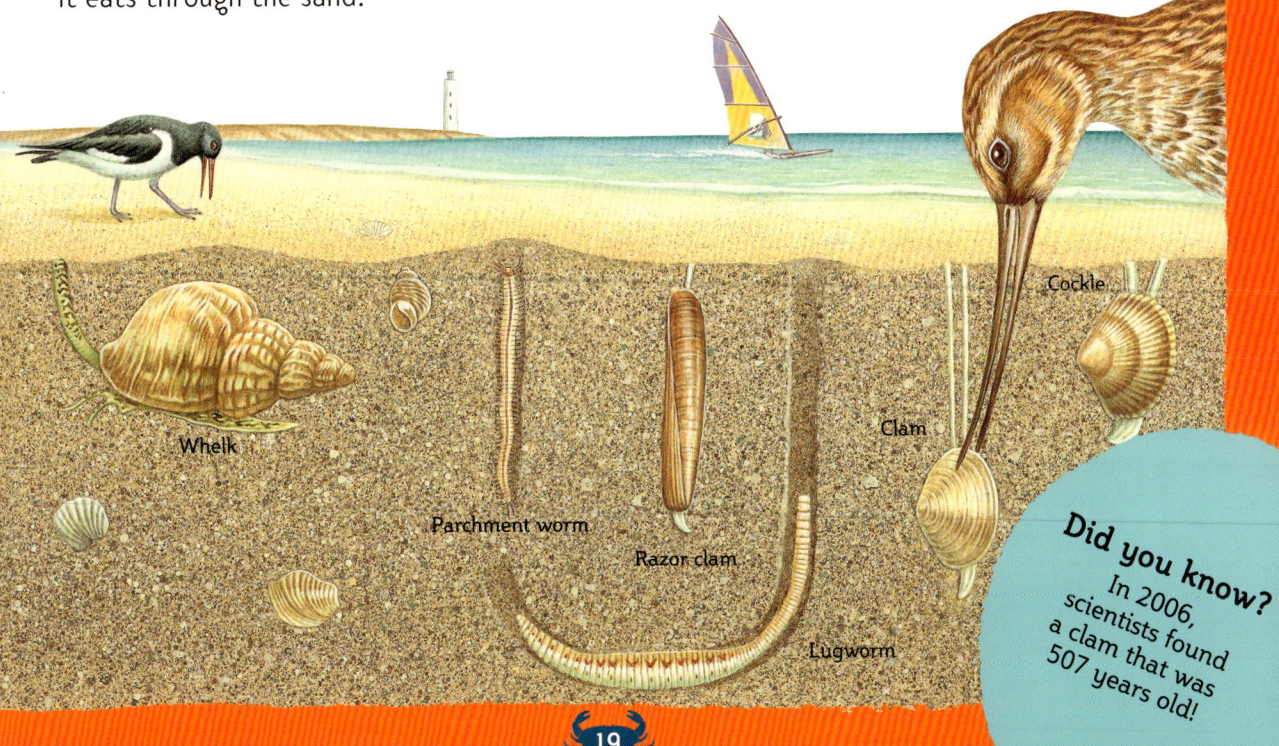

Whelk

Parchment worm

Razor clam

Clam

Cockle

Lugworm

**Did you know?**
In 2006, scientists found a clam that was 507 years old!

# Why do fish have holes on either of their head?

So they can breathe underwater. The slits on either side of their head, called gills, filter out oxygen from the water they swallow.

Fish eggs

Fin

Scales

Tail

Gills

Fishbones

Fish skeleton

Seahorse

Clownfish

Swordfish

Angelfish

Ocean sunfish

Butterflyfish

Mandarinfish

Manta ray

## Why do **sharks** have so many teeth?

🐠 Sharks have rows and rows of extra teeth because their teeth break or fall out all the time. When this happens, a tooth from the next row takes its place.

## Why do **jellyfish** sting?

🐠 Jellyfish have long tentacles which can inject poison. They sting and paralyse their prey before eating it.

## Why do **flatfish** have both eyes one side of their head?

🐠 Flatfish live on the sea floor. Having both eyes on one side of their head helps them to see better. As they grow into adult fish, one eye moves over to the other side of their head.

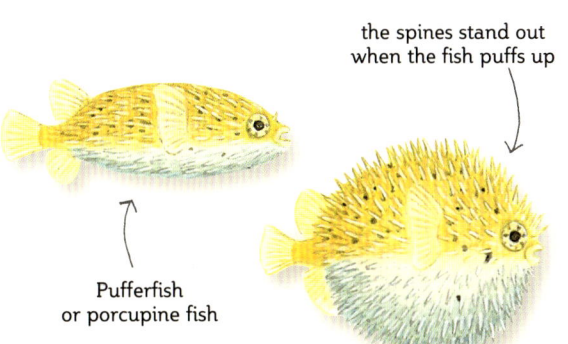

the spines stand out when the fish puffs up

Pufferfish or porcupine fish

## Why does the **pufferfish** blow itself up like a balloon?

🐠 To defend itself! When it feels threatened, the pufferfish's body fills with water, and its pointed spines stand out. Some are also very poinonous!

## Why do sperm whales have so many scars?

Sperm whales feed on squid. They will dive to depths of up to 2,000 metres (6,600 ft) to catch their prey. The giant squid at the bottom of the sea put up a fierce fight and leave their mark on the whale.

## Why do dolphins come to the surface of the water to breathe?

Dolphins are mammals like us, so they can't breathe underwater as fish do. However, they can stay underwater for 15 minutes before coming up for air.

Gannet

Black-headed gull

## Why do **seabirds** dive-bomb into the sea?

🐟 To catch fish. Gannets can spot shoals of fish from the air and dive-bomb to depths of 7 metres (23 ft) under the water to catch their prey.

## Why do **whales** have blowholes?

🐟 Whales need to come up to the surface to breathe. They blow the air out of their lungs as they reach the surface and this produces a great spray of water droplets, called a 'blow'.

**Did you know?** Dolphins can jump as high as 4 m (13 ft) out of the water!

## Why do boats float?

🐟 Boats float because they are lighter than water. An object floats in water if it weighs less than the volume of water it displaces, or moves out the way.

## Why do submarines go underwater?

🐟 This is what they are built to do. Submarines are used by the navy to move around without being seen. Scientists use them to explore the ocean floor.

**Did you know?** Marine research submarines can dive to depths of 3,000 m (9,800 ft).

## Why are there so many fishing knots?

Each knot is used for a particular task, like tying a boat up on the quayside. A good knot should not come undone, even if pulled very hard, and it should always be easy to undo.

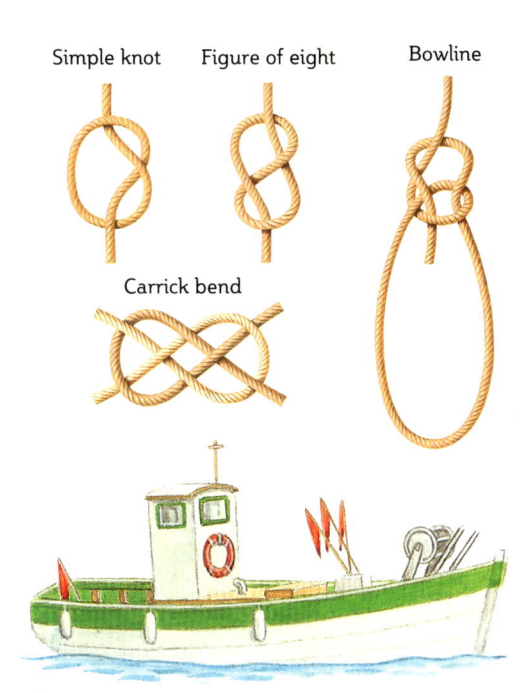

Simple knot   Figure of eight   Bowline

Carrick bend

Clove hitch

**1** Make a loop.

**2** Make a second loop.

**3** Slide both loops over the post.

**4** Pull the two ends tight.

## Why do fishermen catch fish?

So we can eat them! Over time fishermen have found ways to catch more and more fish. But there are now strict laws in place to prevent overfishing and to maintain the numbers of fish in the sea.

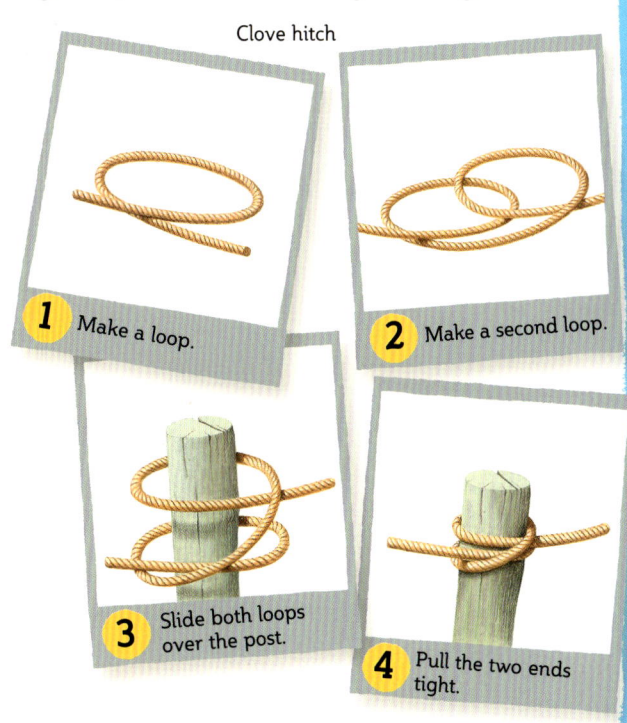

## Why are goods transported by ship?

Shipping is a practical way of transporting large quantities of goods over long distances. The goods are loaded into huge metal containers and stacked one on top of the other.

# The mountains

**Why are there hardly any trees at the top of mountains?**

The higher up you go, the colder it gets and the more difficult it is for trees and other plants to grow. There are no trees on high mountaintops, just moss and bare rock.

**Why are mountain peaks covered in snow in summer?**

Even when the Sun is shining in summer, it is very cold at the top of mountains. The higher the peaks are, the more snow there is. The snow never melts on some peaks.

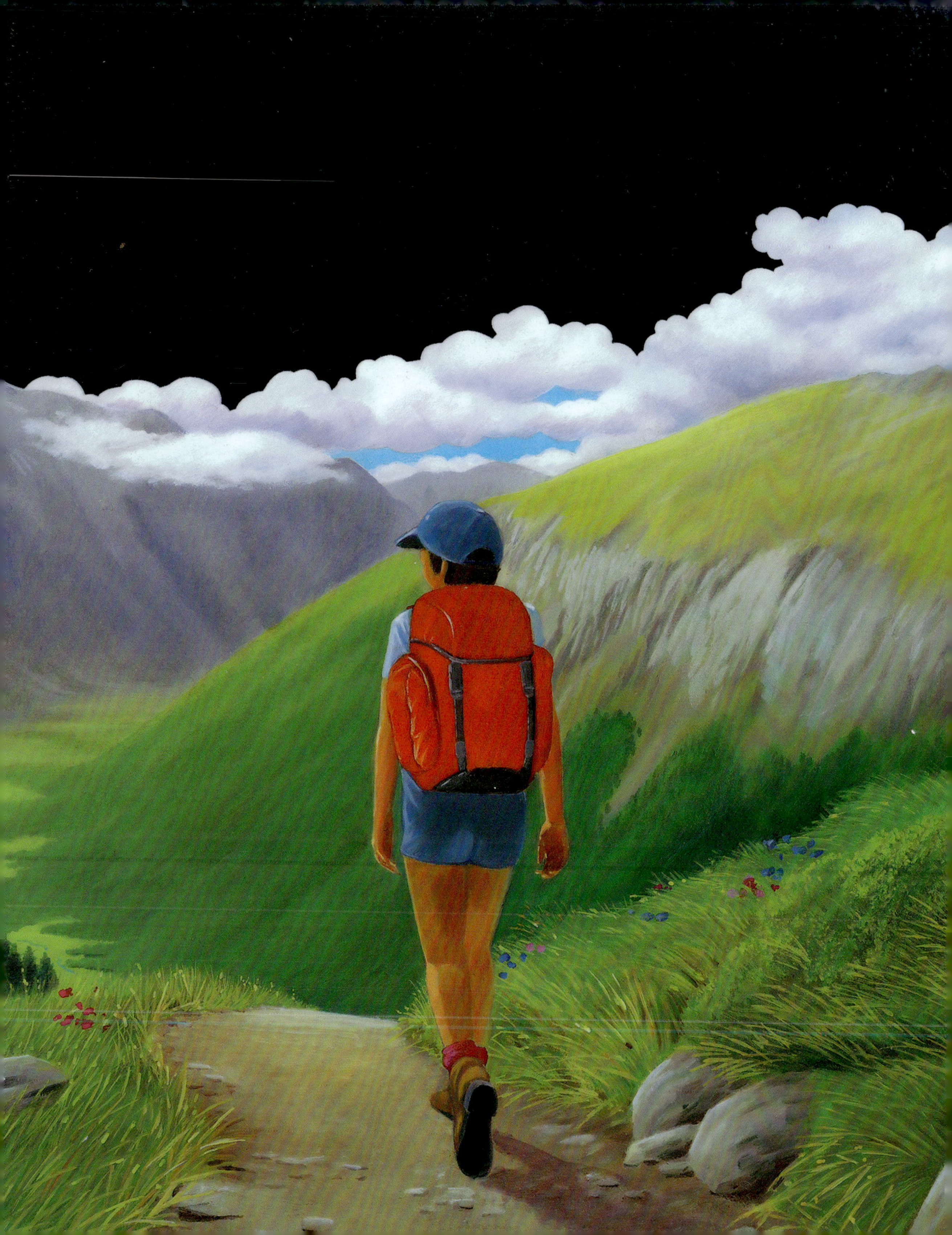

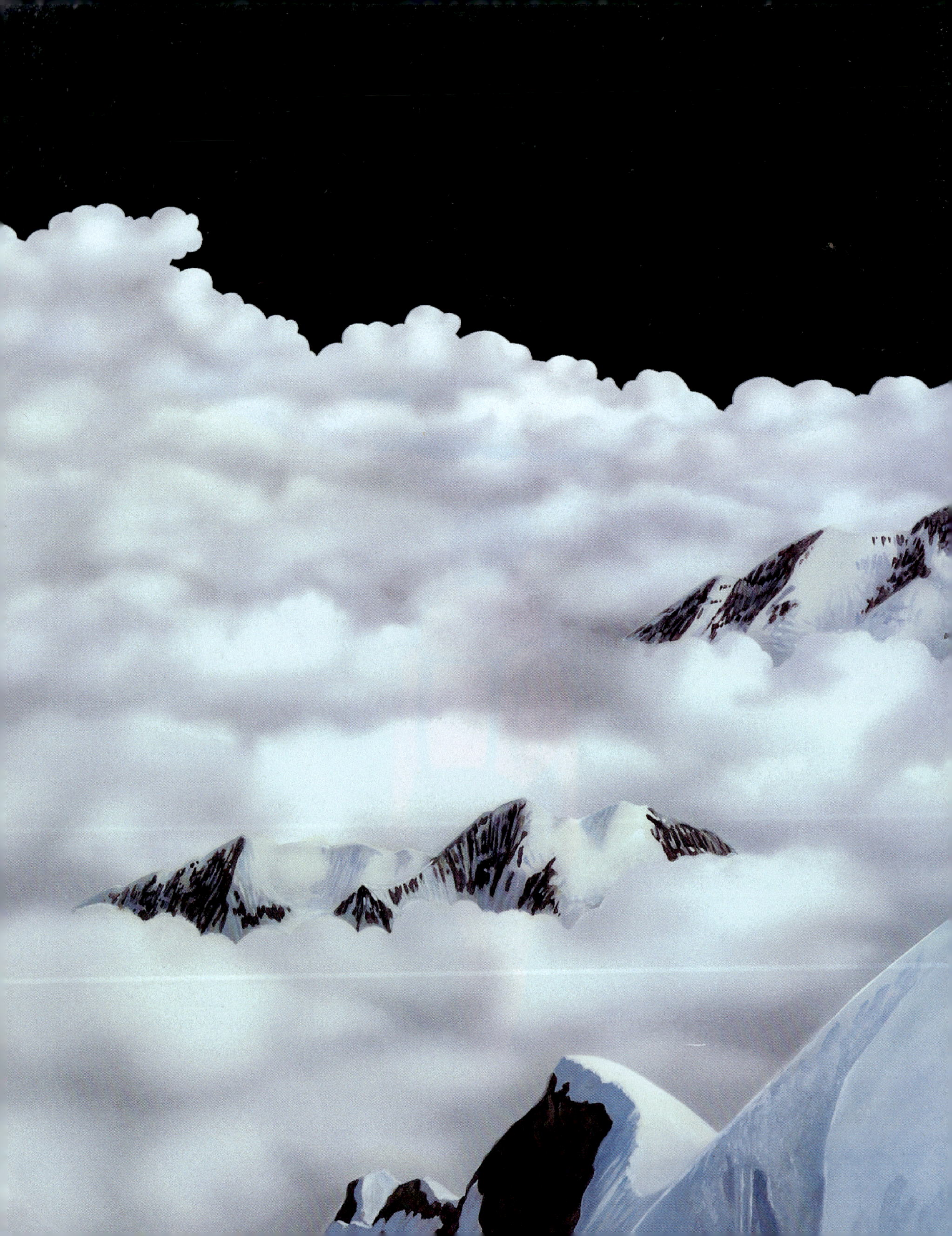

Go for a walk in the mountains and see how different everything is. It's colder, there's snow, pine forests, meadows of wild flowers. Listen out for cowbells, a marmot whistling. Look carefully and you may even see a mountain goat or an eagle.

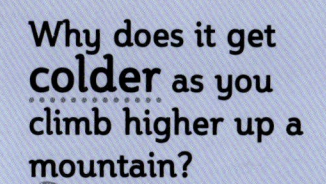

## Why does it get colder as you climb higher up a mountain?

The higher you climb the less air there is. As the air pressure goes down, so does the temperature. The temperature drops about 1 °C for every 100 metres (330 ft) you climb.

## Why do some climbers wear masks at high altitudes?

Where there is less air, there is less oxygen. Without an oxygen mask, mountaineers find it hard to breathe, their heads ache and they may even lose consciousness.

## Why are **mountain streams** so full in the spring?

In spring, fast-flowing streams run out from under the melting snow on the mountains. They cascade down the steep slopes into the valley below.

## Why are there so many **pine trees** in the mountains?

Pine trees are well-suited to cold conditions. Their needles retain moisture and their branches are supple, so that the snow slips off them easily.

## Why are there **mountains**?

The surface of the Earth is made up of huge plates. When two plates collide, one sinks down while the other rises up in great folds, producing mountains.

## Why do some mountains have strange shapes?

Mountains get worn down over time by what we call erosion. This can be caused by water running down the slopes, by ice, by the wind or by extremes of temperature.

## Why do volcanoes form mountains?

When volcanoes erupt, they spew out red-hot, molten rock, called lava, which cools to form rock. Over time some volcanoes will form a mountain, made up of layer upon layer of lava. However, only a few mountains were once volcanoes.

**Did you know?**
Mauna Kea is the tallest volcano in the world, over 10,000 m (33,000 ft) from top to bottom, but much of it is underwater!

## Why do **eagles** circle round and round in the sky?

Eagles know how to ride currents of rising air with their wings spread wide. Circling effortlessly high in the sky enables them to spot their prey, and to save energy for when they need to hunt.

## Why do **bears** fish in streams?

They catch fish swimming upstream. Fish form a big part of their diet. Normally bears are solitary animals. They live and hunt alone, but they come together to fish.

## Why do **marmots** whistle when you get close?

They whistle to warn other marmots that there is danger nearby. There is always one marmot keeping watch. They are sometimes called 'whistlers'.

## Why do some animals turn **white** in winter?

Some mountain animals, like the North American snowshoe hare, grow white winter coats as camouflage to hide them from predators. Their winter coats are much warmer and thicker than their summer ones.

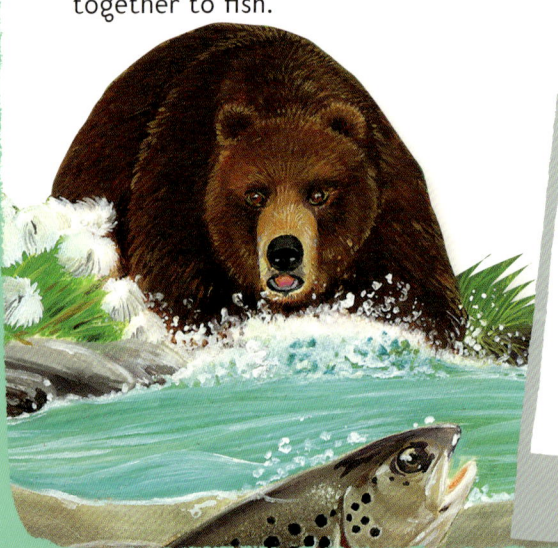

1 Summer coat

2 Winter coat

## Why are there **wolves** in some mountains?

Wolves nearly disappeared from Europe during last century because of hunting, but now they are protected, their populations have increased in parts of Northern and Eastern Europe.

## Why do people **herd** animals up into the mountains for the summer?

So that the sheep and cattle can graze on the rich green pastures during the summer months. They drive them up at the end of May and bring them down again in October.

## Why do some **animals** prefer to live in the mountains?

Because they are well-adapted to the mountains. Chamois and mountain goats have special flexible pads on their hooves which make them very good climbers. They leap from rock to rock without ever losing their balance.

# Why are the **wild flowers** so brightly coloured in the mountains?

The bright colours and unusual shapes of the flowers attract insects, which carry pollen from one plant to another, enabling them to reproduce. There are fewer insects in the mountains, so attracting them is particularly important!

Chicory

Edelweiss

Pepper saxifrage

Stitchwort

Geranium

Violet

Forget-me-not

Pansy

Red dead-nettle

Gentian

Lady's smock

Campanula

Cowslip

Speedwell

### Why does it snow?

Water turns into ice in the cold. In winter, when the temperature is near freezing (0 °C), water droplets falling from clouds turn into snowflakes before they hit the ground.

### Why do we slide on snow?

We think we slide on snow but we actually slide on a thin film of water. This forms on the surface of the snow under our feet as the weight of our body pushes down on it.

### Why are no two snowflakes ever the same?

Each snowflake consists of a series of little crystals which stick together as they fall. Some melt a little on their way down, others are thicker. No two are ever the same.

## Why do **crevasses** form in glaciers?

Glaciers are thick layers of very hard snow and ice which move slowly downhill. As they move down the mountain over uneven ground, they break up, producing deep cracks, called crevasses.

## Why are there **avalanches** in the mountains?

When fresh snow falls on top of a hard layer of compacted snow, the fresh layer of snow sometimes breaks loose and begins to slide down the mountain, gathering speed and taking everything with it as it goes.

**Did you know?** Mount Everest is the tallest mountain in the world at 8,848 m (29,030 ft).

## Why do people choose to **live** in the mountains?

People are attracted by the outdoor way of life and the contact with nature. They enjoy the walking, skiing, snowboarding, climbing and other activities you can do in mountains. There are ski resorts in many moutain areas.

## Why do people dig **tunnels**?

Tunnels link two places together. Underground tunnels can be used for roads, railway lines, or canals.

## Why do people build **dams**?

Damns are a way of storing water in large reservoirs. The water may be used for drinking, to water crops or to produce electricity.

Helicopter

Peak

Chair lift

Cable car

Tunnel

Ski resort

Lake

Dam

Village

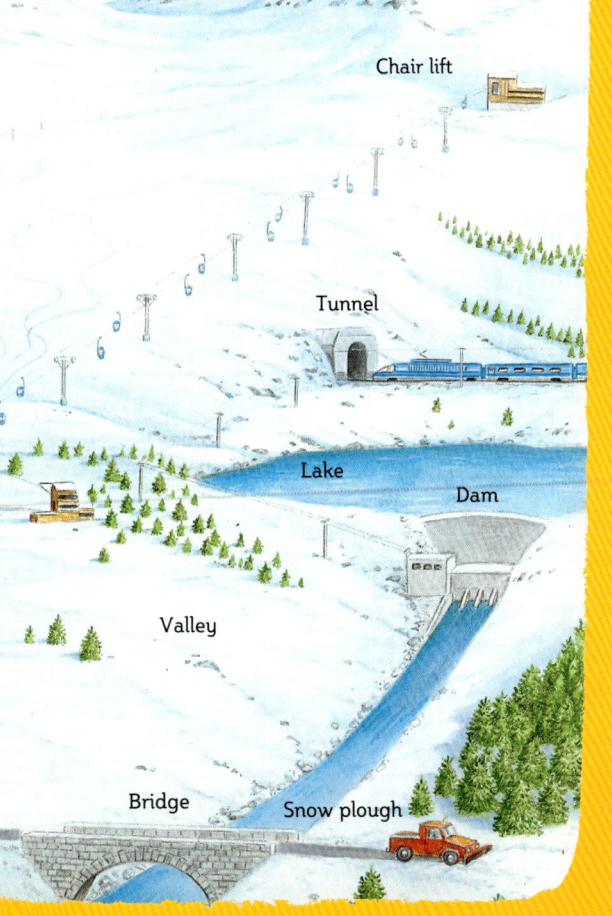

Valley

Bridge

Snow plough

# Animals

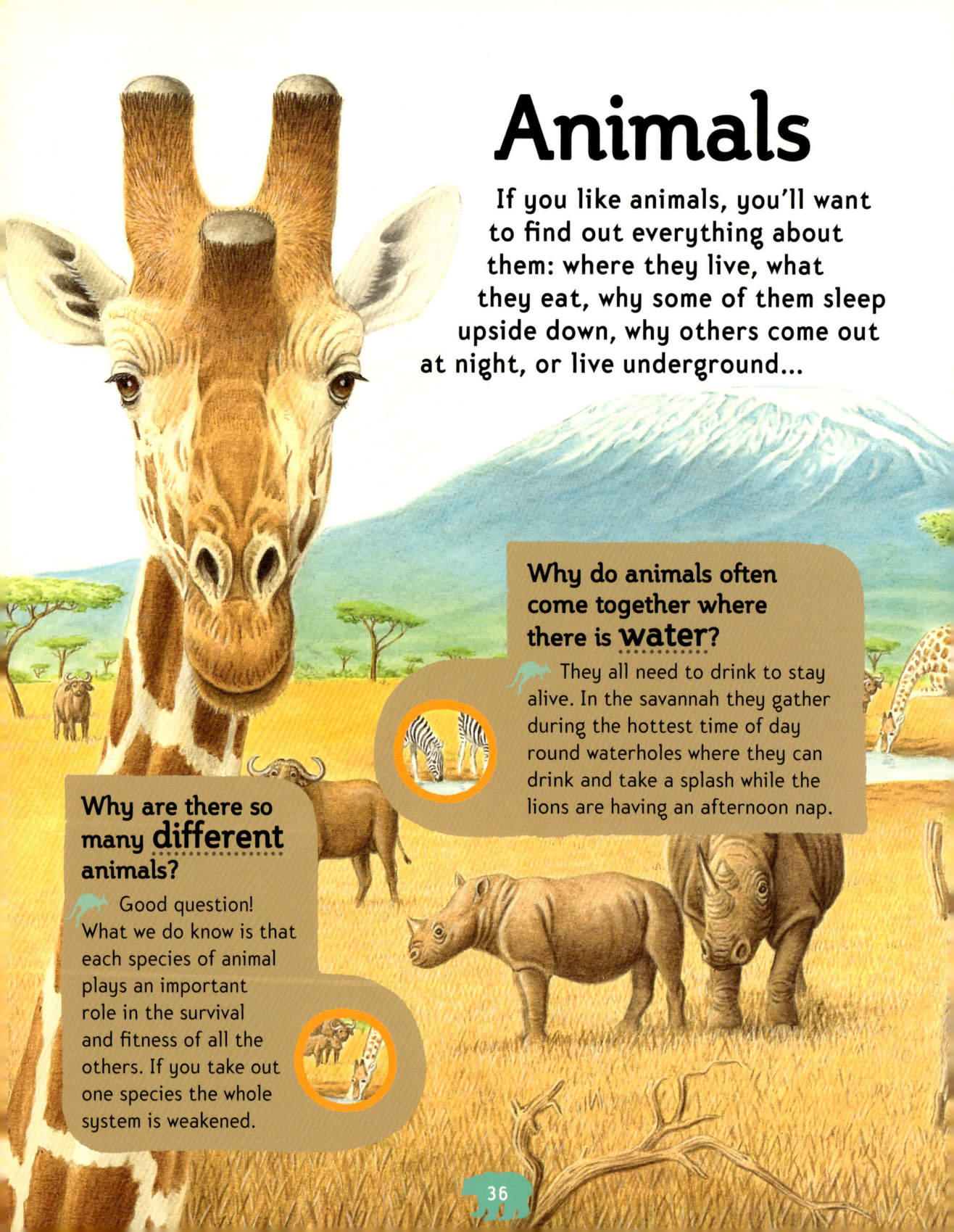

If you like animals, you'll want to find out everything about them: where they live, what they eat, why some of them sleep upside down, why others come out at night, or live underground...

## Why do animals often come together where there is **water**?

They all need to drink to stay alive. In the savannah they gather during the hottest time of day round waterholes where they can drink and take a splash while the lions are having an afternoon nap.

## Why are there so many **different** animals?

Good question! What we do know is that each species of animal plays an important role in the survival and fitness of all the others. If you take out one species the whole system is weakened.

## Why do some animals prefer to come out at night?

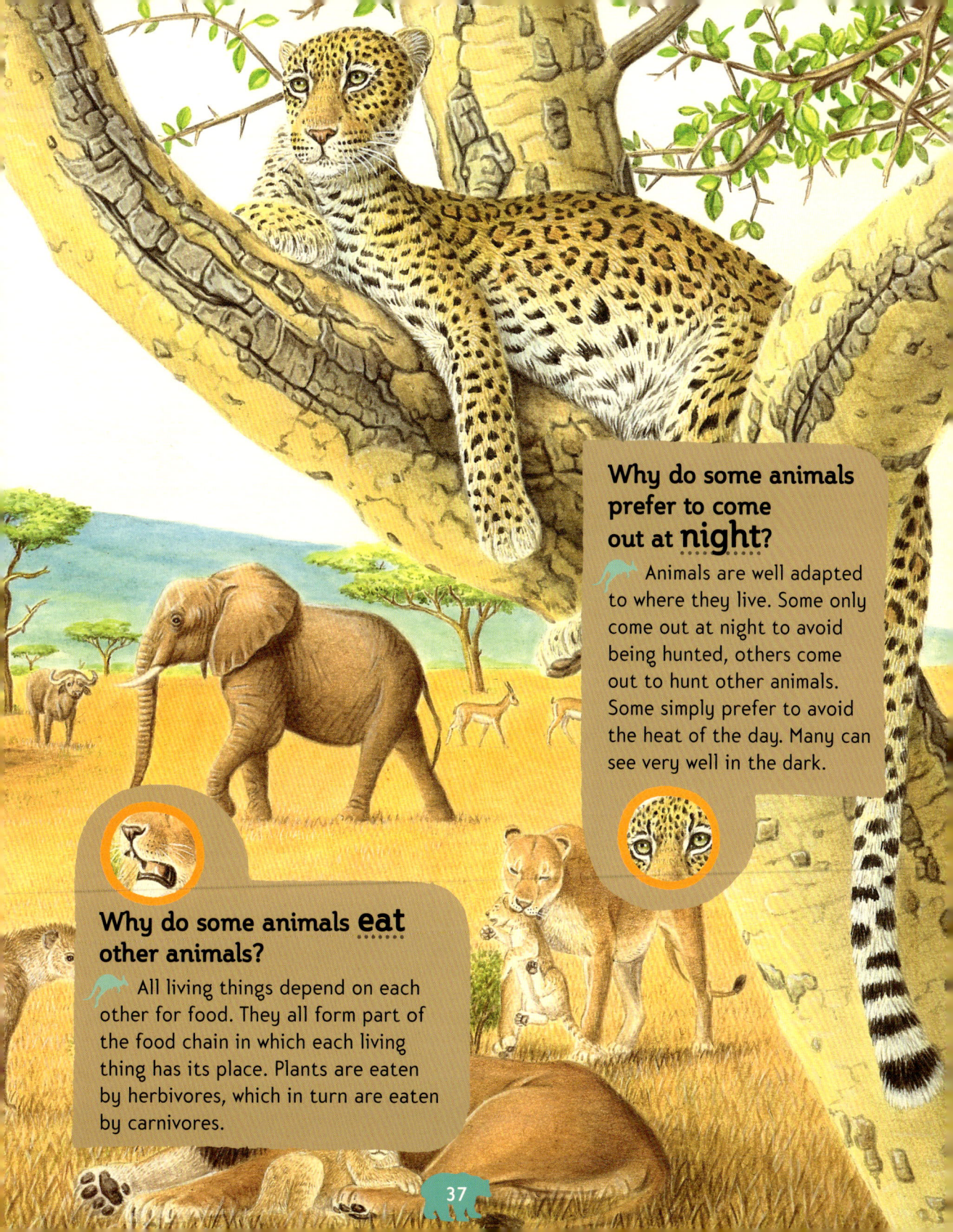

Animals are well adapted to where they live. Some only come out at night to avoid being hunted, others come out to hunt other animals. Some simply prefer to avoid the heat of the day. Many can see very well in the dark.

## Why do some animals eat other animals?

All living things depend on each other for food. They all form part of the food chain in which each living thing has its place. Plants are eaten by herbivores, which in turn are eaten by carnivores.

## Why do elephants hold each other's tails?

🦘 A baby elephant holds on to its mother's tail so that it does not get lost or left behind when the herd is on the move. It will start following its mother two days after it is born.

## Why do we say the lion is the king of the animals?

🦘 Lions' thick manes look a bit like a crown. They are also the biggest hunters on the savannah. A lion may leave the hunting to the lionesses, but it will always be the first to feed.

## Why do zebras have stripes?

🦘 People used to think that stripes made them more difficult for predators to see in the long grass of the savannah, but now scientists think the stripes may help to keep zebras cool and protect them from insect bites.

## Why do giraffes have such long necks?

🦘 To reach leaves high up in trees. Over time, giraffes with longer necks found food more easily and had more babies than shorter-necked giraffes. Their babies were also born with long necks!

# Why do **parrots** copy what you say?

🦘 Copying sounds is a means of self-defence. Parrots are naturally good mimics. They warn other parrots of danger and keep predators at bay by imitating their cries.

## Exotic birds

Humming bird

Rainbow lorikeet

Rosella

Hyacinth macaw

Galah

Toucan

Scarlet macaw

Eye with broad vision

Powerful beak

African grey parrot

Cockatoo

Blue and yellow macaw

Stiff black tongue

Strong and agile feet

## Why do **dromedaries** have humps?

🦘 Fatty tissue stored in the dromedary's hump allows it to go long distances without eating or drinking. Dromedaries live in Africa and have one hump. Camels live in deserts in Asia where nights are much colder. They have two humps.

## Why do **tortoises** move so slowly?

🦘 The weight of their shell and their very short legs makes it hard for tortoises to move fast. They don't need to hurry because wherever they are, they can always take cover inside their thick shells.

## Why don't **snakes** have legs?

🦘 Over time snakes evolved a different way of moving around. By using the scale on their bellies to grip the soil, they can glide very fast over the ground.

Desert fox

Jerboa

Adder

Scorpion

Lizard

Ants

## Why do animals hide underground in the **desert**?

🦘 To escape the heat. They spend most of the day underground and come out at night when it's cooler. In milder climates it's the the other way round. Animals go underground at night to escape the cold.

## Why are **polar bears** white?

Being white makes them difficult to spot on the ice floe when they are hunting. They can creep up on seals more easily and surprise them. Under the fur their skin is black, which conserves heat.

North Pole

## Why do **reindeer** have antlers?

Antlers are good protection in a fight. They also act as antennae, making it easier for the reindeer to hear. Females have smaller antlers, which fall off and grow again each year.

South Pole

## Why do baby **penguins** perch on their parents' feet?

That way the baby penguins keep warm in the freezing cold of the winter months. Temperatures can drop to -40° C in the Antarctic. They perch on their parents' feet until they are 8 months old.

**Did you know?** The largest living species of penguin is the Emperor Penguin.

## Why do **chicks** come from eggs?

Hens lay eggs and sit on them. Inside the egg the chick develops. After 20 days it cracks open the eggshell with its beak.

**1** The embryo develops.

**2** The chick is ready to hatch.

**3** Once it dries out, it's fluffy and soft.

## Why does a **rabbit's** nose keep twitching?

So they can smell better. Rabbits use their strong sense of smell for everything: to find food, to detect intruders, and to sense danger.

## Why do **cows** produce milk?

Cows start producing milk when they have a calf. Provided a cow has one calf a year, and is milked each day, it will go on producing milk all year round for years.

**Did you know?**
One milking cow produces 20 litres of milk a day!

42

## Why do swallows return every year in the spring?

🦘 Swallows return every year to mate, build nests and rear their babies. In the autumn they fly back to Africa to spend the winter in a warmer cimate.

## Why do cats always fall on their feet?

🦘 Cats get their extraordinary sense of balance from their ancestors who lived and hunted in trees. When they fall, they instinctively turn in the air and land on their feet.

## Why does a dog wag its tail?

🦘 A dog's tail is part of its backbone. It start wagging whenever the dog gets excited, and not just when it's happy.

### Why did dinosaurs disappear?

Scientists think a big meteorite crashed into the Earth from space. This set up a huge cloud of dust that blocked out the Sun for a long period. Without sunlight, the Earth got colder and many creatures died.

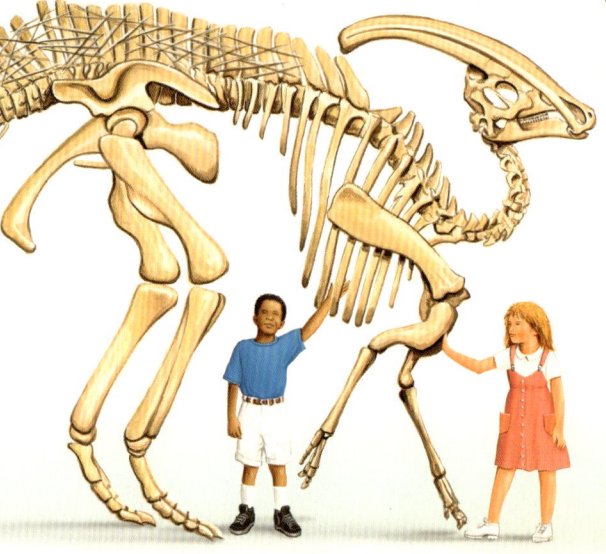

### Why are flamingoes pink?

Because they eat so many shrimps. The shrimps are pink because they feed on pink algae. If a flamingo stops eating shrimps, it turns grey.

### Why are there so few pandas?

Pandas very seldom produce any young in captivity, and they are disappearing in the wild. They feed almost entirely on bamboo. Where they live in China, the forests of bamboo they feed on are being cut down.

## Why do **bats** sleep upside down?

Bats' back legs are too weak for them to take off from the ground. They sleep hanging upside down so that when they wake they can simply release their grip, unfold their wings and fly away safely.

## Why do **chameleons** change colour?

Chameleons change colour to merge with their surroundings. This helps them hide from predators. Colour is also a signal to other chameleons. They turn grey when frightened, green when they are at ease.

## Why do mother **kangaroos** have pouches?

A kangaroo's pouch is a warm, safe place to travel. Baby kangaroos start leaving their mother's pouches for short spells at six months, but return to feed and sleep with their mothers until they are a year old.

### Did you know?
Kangaroos can jump as far as 13 m (43 ft) in a single hop, and up to 3.5 m (12 ft) up in the air.

# Our body

We all have a body. How much do you know about yours? How does it work? Why is it that for some things you can make it do what you want, and for other things your body decides for you? Maybe it's time to find out!

### Why do we each have a name?

Names make it easier to identify each of us. Our surnames tell us which family we belong to. Our first names, given to us by our parents, mean we all have different names within the family.

### Why do children grow?

Our bodies are programmed to grow. They produce special growth hormones to help us grow and change, especially during our teenage years. Girls stop growing at about 16. Boys go on growing until they are 22.

## Why are we each different?

Humans adapt to their environment. For example, people's skin colour is darker in countries where it is very hot. We also inherit different features from each of our parents.

## Why are there boys and girls?

So that people can have children! Reproduction is essential for the survival of all species, including humans. There are roughly the same number of men as women in the world.

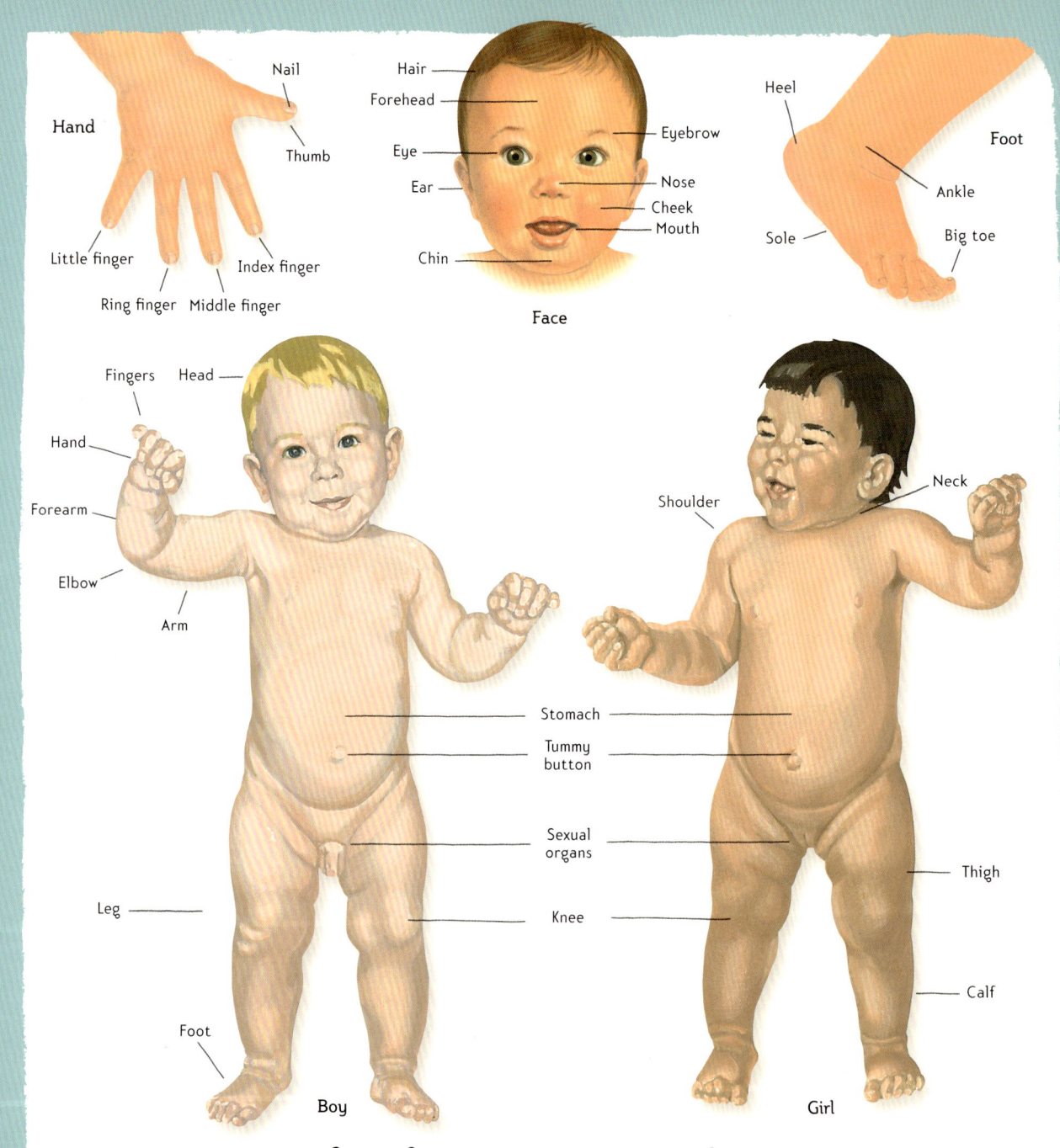

**Hand**: Nail, Thumb, Little finger, Ring finger, Middle finger, Index finger

**Face**: Hair, Forehead, Eye, Ear, Chin, Eyebrow, Nose, Cheek, Mouth

**Foot**: Heel, Sole, Ankle, Big toe

**Boy**: Fingers, Head, Hand, Forearm, Elbow, Arm, Leg, Foot, Stomach, Tummy button, Sexual organs, Knee

**Girl**: Shoulder, Neck, Thigh, Calf

## Why do we have a head, a torso, arms and legs?

We have a head for thinking and perceiving, arms to grip and make things, legs to stand on and walk, and a torso to hold it all together and to house important organs like the heart.

## Why do we have bones?

To keep us upright. Without bones we would be all floppy, like slugs. Our bones come together to form a skeleton. There are 206 bones in the human body.

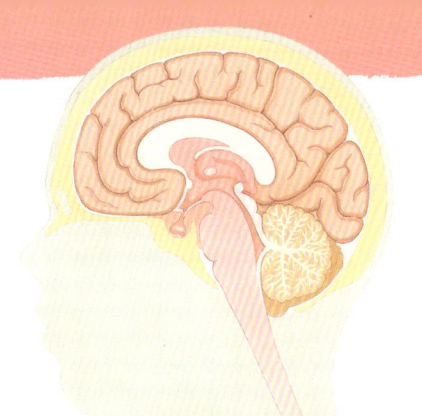

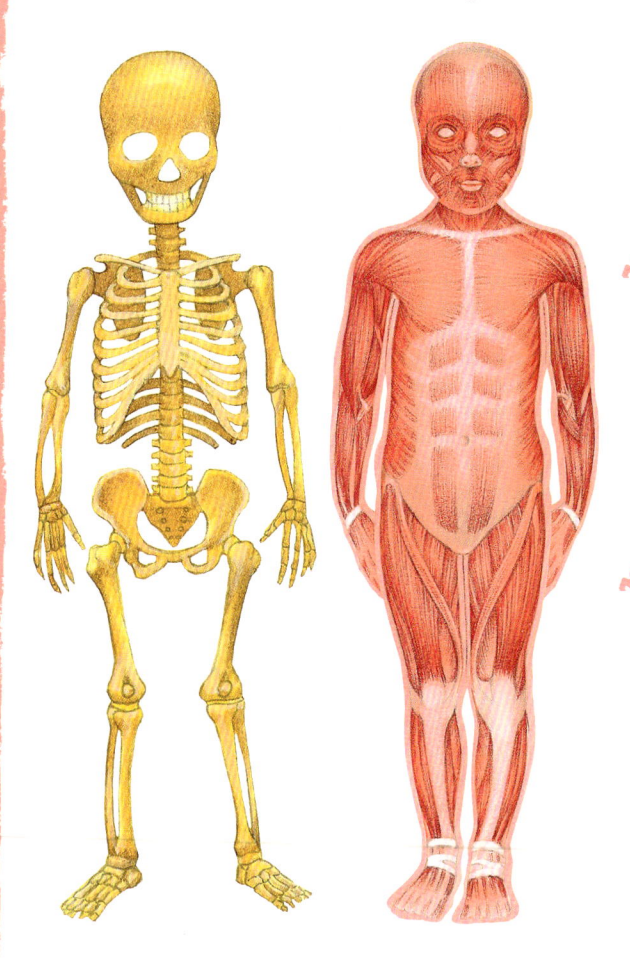

## Why do we have thoughts in our heads?

Because we have brains, composed of billions of cells. These brain cells react each time something happens to us, and they send messages to all the different parts of our body.

## Why is our body covered in skin?

Our skin is a barrier between our body and the outside world. It protects us, helps maintain our body temperature and tells us if something is hot or cold, soft or hard, comfortable or painful.

## Why do we have muscles?

Muscles help us walk, run, speak, scratch our heads. Muscles are what make our bodies move. Humans have 700 different muscles. Most of them are attached to our bones by tendons.

## Why can't we eat just one sort of food?

The body needs a variety of different types of food to stay healthy. Meat and fish help our cells regenerate, fruit and vegetables give us vital vitamins. Nuts are good for our heart.

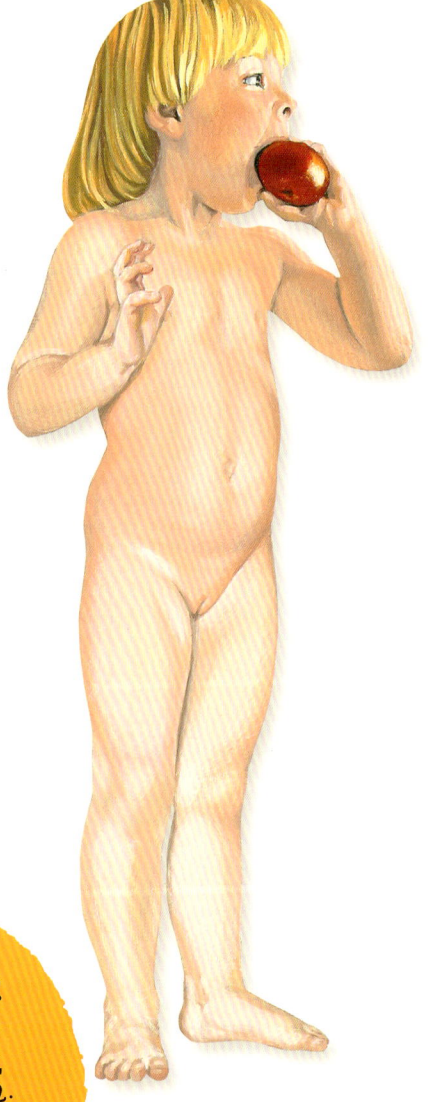

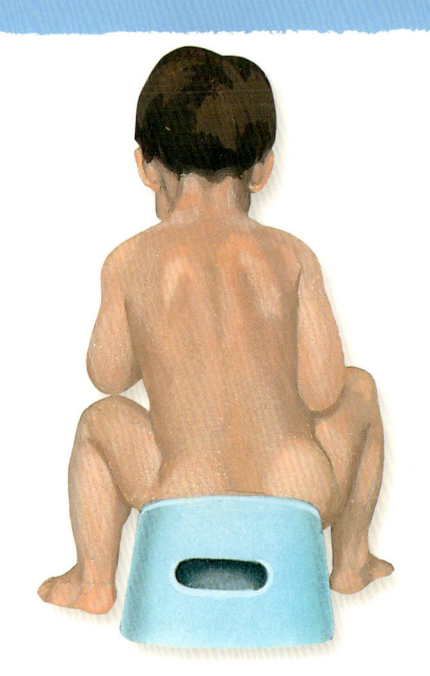

## Why do we pee and poo?

To get rid of waste our bodies don't need: food waste, but also bacteria which help break down the food in our stomach.

## Why do we lose our teeth?

Milk teeth are the small teeth children have up to the age of 6. They fall out and adult teeth that are larger and stonger take their place.

**Did you know?** Small children have 20 teeth, and adults 32.

## Why do we breathe?

Breathing keeps us alive. Oxygen from the air we breathe in passes into our blood through our lungs. It is pumped around our body by the heart, giving it energy. Part of the air we breathe in goes back out the way it came in.

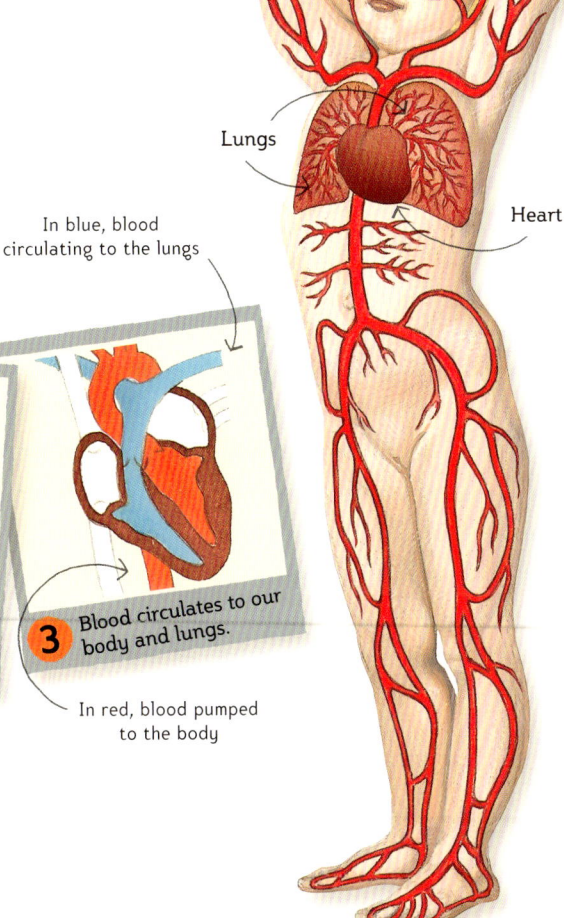

## Why do we sleep?

To rest our body and mind. Sleep helps our brain digest the day's experiences. It is also the time children's bodies grow the fastest.

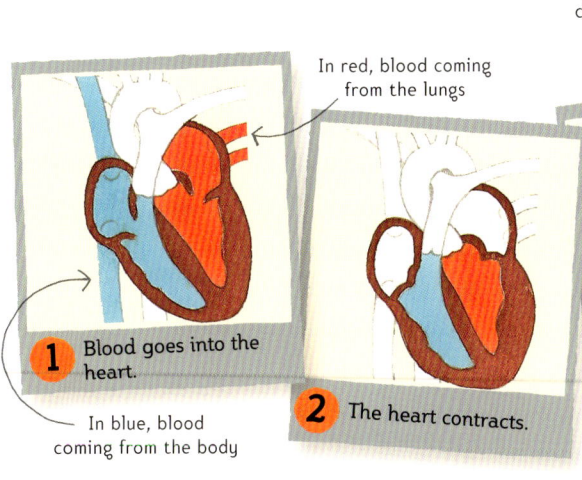

Lungs

Heart

In blue, blood circulating to the lungs

In red, blood coming from the lungs

1. Blood goes into the heart.
   - In blue, blood coming from the body
2. The heart contracts.
3. Blood circulates to our body and lungs.
   - In red, blood pumped to the body

## Why does our heart beat?

The heart is a muscle. It beats to pump blood full of oxygen coming from the lungs. Then it sends it to the organs which need it for energy. When resting the heart beats 70 times a minute on average.

① We hear with our ears.

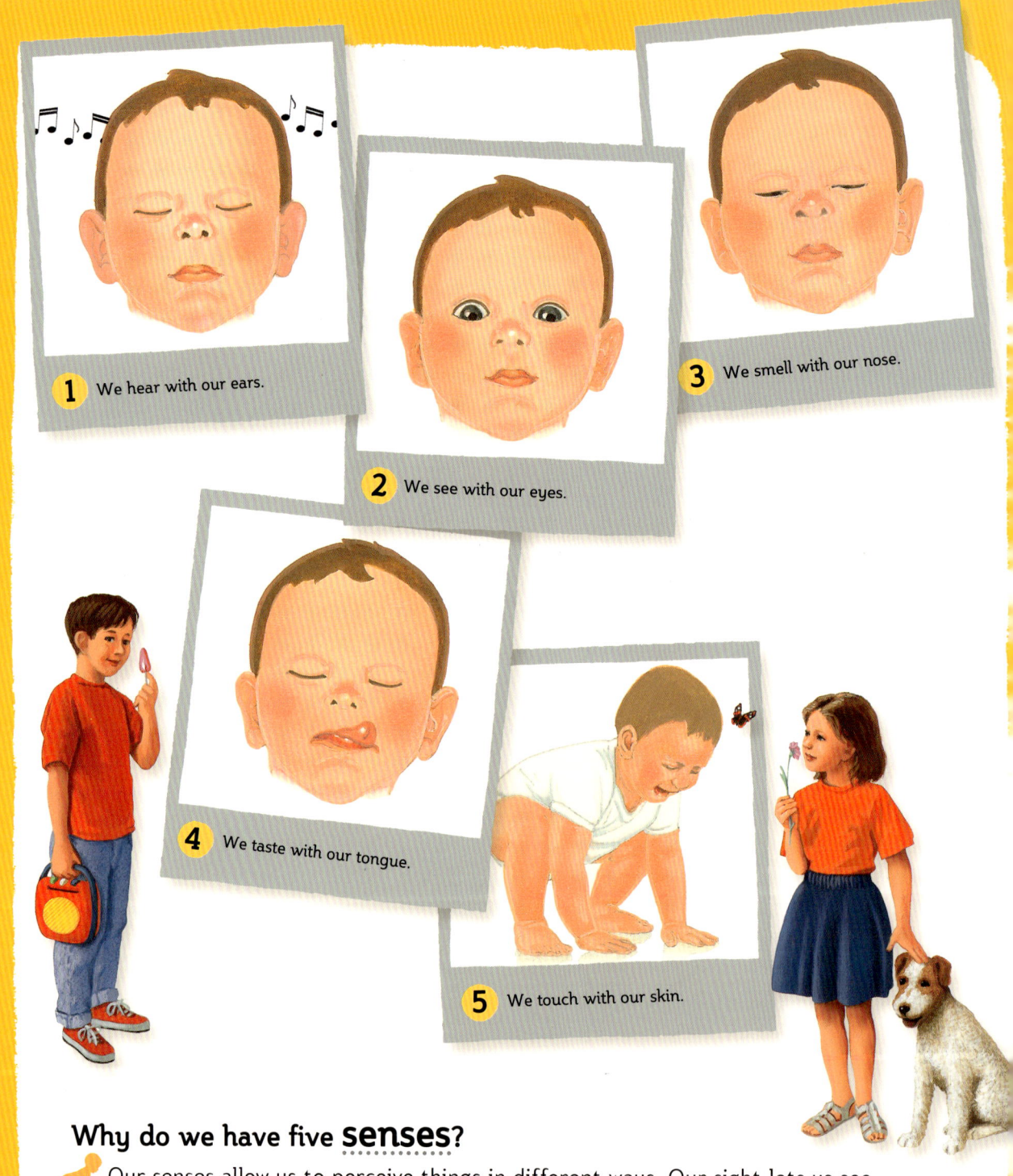

② We see with our eyes.

③ We smell with our nose.

④ We taste with our tongue.

⑤ We touch with our skin.

## Why do we have five senses?

Our senses allow us to perceive things in different ways. Our sight lets us see, hearing allows us to listen. We have a nose to smell things, our skin allows us to touch things and our tongue to taste things.

## Why do we dream?

Dreams are strange things. They can be scary, or a bit crazy. While we sleep, part of our brain is busy sorting and organising memories and impressions we receive during our waking hours.

## Why do we laugh?

We laugh when we are feeling happy, surprised or nervous. Laughter is one way our body uses to express emotions. Children up to the age of 6 laugh the most.

## Why do we cry?

Tears are a sign of pain or distress. Sometimes people cry when they are happy. Like laughter, they are a way we express what we feel. Some people cry more than others.

1 A small cell...

2 A fetus at one month

3 At a month and a half

4 At three months

5 At five months

## Why do babies spend such a long time in their mother's tummies?

Babies spend 9 months developing in the mother's tummy to be able to live outside it. When a baby is born too early, it can be very weak and may need hospital care to survive.

## Why do we have tummy buttons?

We all start life in our mother's tummy. Before we are born, we get food and oxygen through a cord which links us to our mother. At birth the cord is cut. Our tummy button is what is left from the cord.

## Why do mummies have babies?

In almost all animal species, the females are the ones who give birth to the babies, and ensure we reproduce, but mummies cannot make babies without the help of daddies!

Grandparents

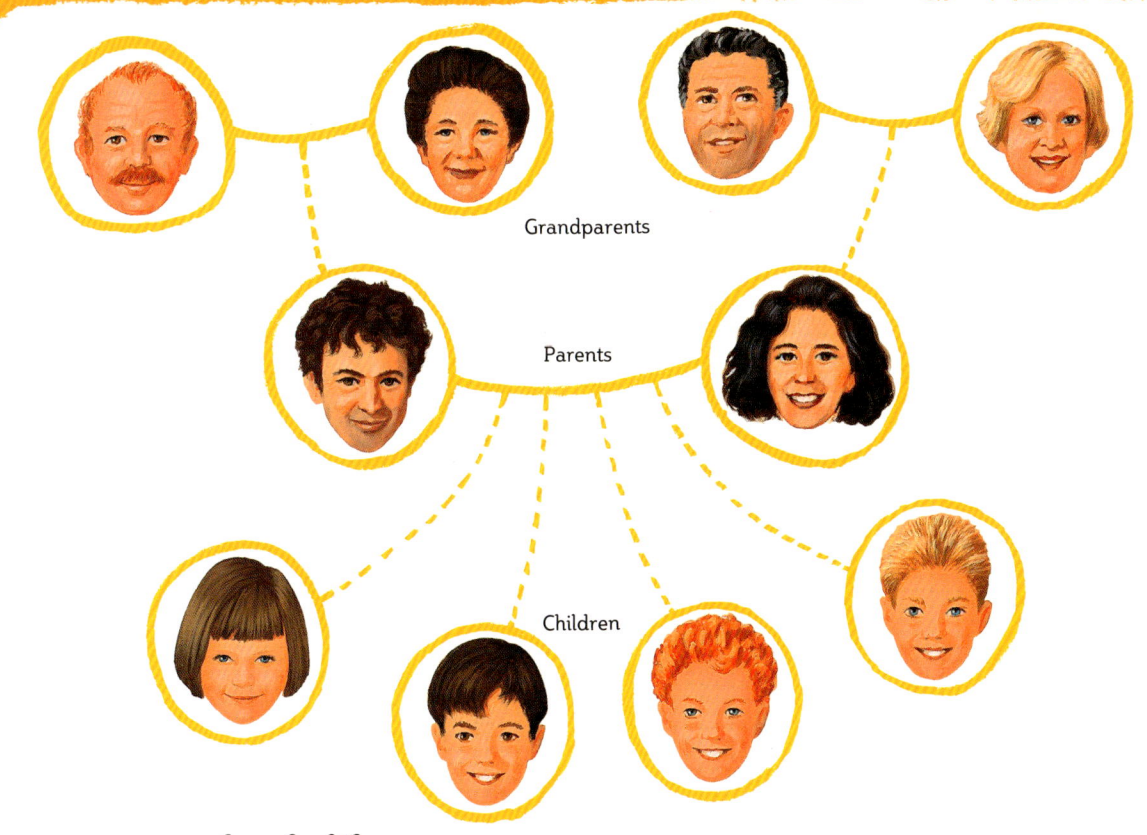

Parents

Children

## Why do we **look like** our parents?

As our body grows and develops, it follows a plan, called a genetic code that tells it how to grow. Some of this plan comes from our father and some from our mother, so we develop features, like the colour of our skin, hair or eyes which are similar to theirs.

## Why can't babies **walk**?

Babies are not strong enough to start walking when they are born. Their brain needs to develop before they can control the muscles involved. Most babies learn to walk between the ages of 12 and 18 months.

**Did you know?**
Most women give birth to their babies between the ages of 18 and 45.

# Earth and sky

The world we live in is amazing. The Earth is round, but we still manage to stand on its surface, wherever we are. It rotates, but we don't fall off. As for the sky, did you know that sunlight is made up of all the colours of the rainbow and that shooting stars are not stars at all?

## Why are there rivers?

In the mountains, rain and melting snow become fast-flowing streams. When they reach the valley, streams turn into rivers, which get wider and slower as they join other rivers.

## Why are we able to live on Earth?

Because there is water, oxygen and a climate that is neither too hot nor too cold. These are the conditions that make life possible on Earth, and no other planet we know of provides them.

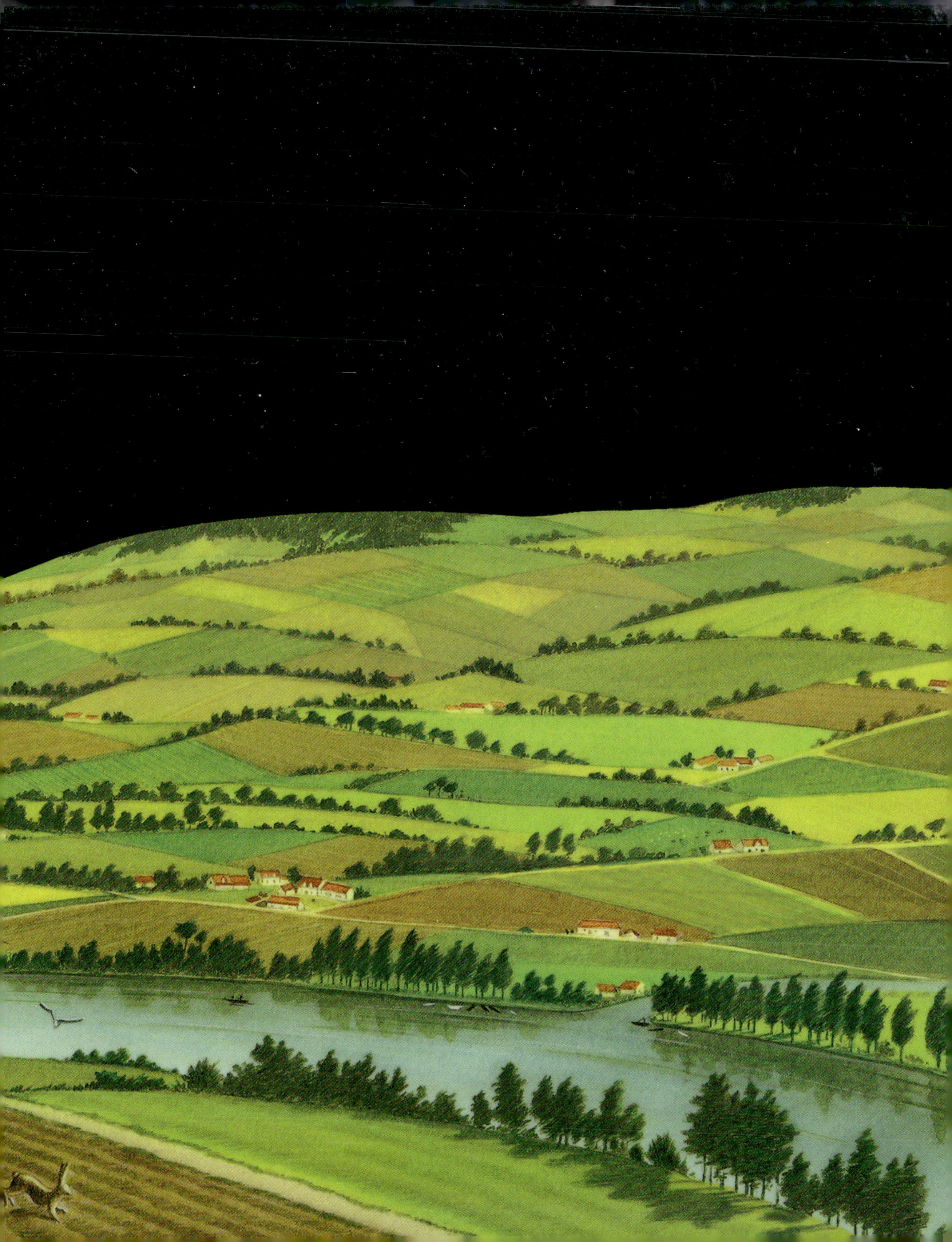

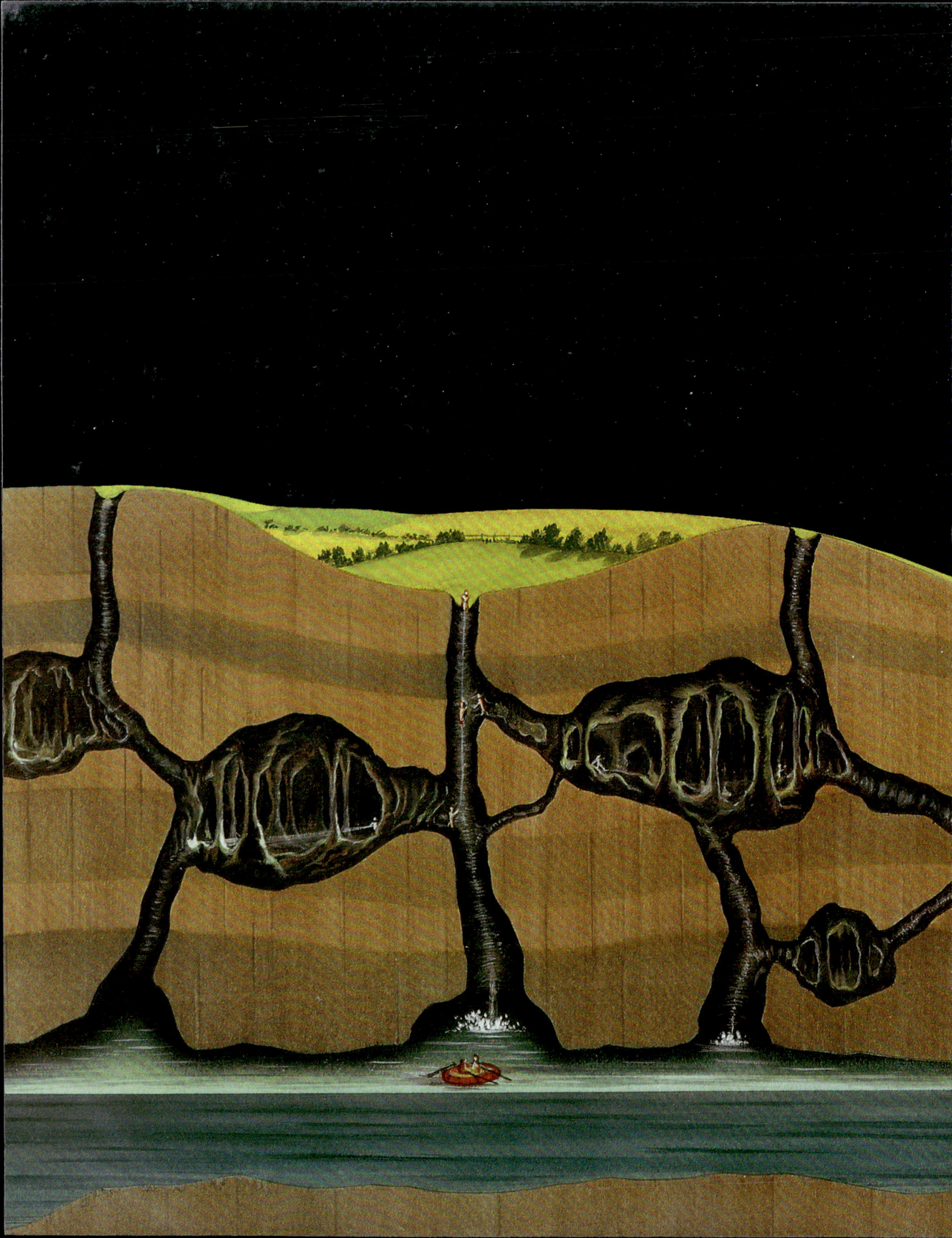

## Why are there underground caves?

Where there is limestone, rainwater passing through it gradually hollows out holes in the rock below the surface. This happens over thousands of years.

## Why is the sky blue?

Sunlight contains all the colours of the rainbow. This mix looks white to us, but when the Sun's rays enter the Earth's atmosphere, the blue light is scattered more than any other colour, so the sky looks blue to us.

## Why do people call the Earth the blue planet?

🌐 Seen from space, the Earth looks completely blue because most of it is covered with water. Three quarters of its surface is covered with oceans, seas, lakes and rivers.

## Why don't we fall off the Earth?

🌐 The Earth is round like a ball, it doesn't have a top or bottom, or a right or wrong side. Wherever we are, in England or Australia, or at the poles, we are drawn to its centre by the force of gravity.

## Why is the Earth round?

🌐 At the beginning there were just specks of dust flying around in space, which began sticking together. They were all drawn to a centre point as if by a magnet, and turned into a ball. This went on getting bigger and bigger until it became the Earth.

**1** Day

**2** Night

## Why do we have day and night?

🌐 The Earth is constantly rotating on its axis. It takes 24 hours to complete one rotation. As the Earth turns, the side nearest the Sun is in light and the other side is in darkness. That is what gives us night and day.

**Did you know?** The Earth rotates in a counter-clockwise direction.

## Winter

January  | February  | March

## Spring

April  | May  | June

## Summer

July  | August  | September

## Autumn

October  | November  | December

## Why do we have seasons?

The Earth revolves around the Sun each year and tilts to one side as it turns. When the part where we live tilts towards the Sun, we receive more direct sunlight, and it is summer. When it tilts away from the Sun, we receive less sunlight, and it is winter.

### Why is it so cold at the poles?

🌐 The poles are cold because they don't get any direct sunlight. The Sun is always low in the sky in summer and never rises above the horizen in winter, so it is cold and dark for months on end.

### Why does lava erupt from volcanoes?

🌐 Volcanoes open downwards to pools of magma: red-hot molten rock and gas, found deep inside the Earth. When the pressure builds up, magma erupts up from the crater in the form of lava.

### Why is there sand in the desert?

🌐 Sand consists of thousands of tiny rock fragments. The force of the wind and big variations in temperature between day and night wear down the rocks until they are reduced to grains of sand.

## Why are there **stalactites** and **stalagmites** in caves?

🌍 Water dripping through the ceiling of caves leaves calcium deposits which slowly build up to make pointed rock formations. They are stalagmites when they form on the ceiling, and stalactites when they form on the floor.

## Why is there water **underground**?

🌍 When it rains water flows over the surface of the Earth, but it also soaks into the ground, where it can form caves, underground rivers and water deposits, called aquifers.

## Why did prehistoric people make **cave paintings**?

🌍 Our ancient ancesters may have thought the paintings had magical powers. Often hidden away, the caves were probably sacred places for special ceremonies.

## Why are **storms** so noisy?

In big storm clouds, air currents cause droplets of water to bump against each other. Electricity builds up and there are flashes of lightning and thunder. The thunder is the sound lightning makes.

## Why are there **clouds**?

Water in seas and rivers evaporates into the air in warm weather. As the water vapour rises into the sky, it meets colder air, and condenses into clusters of tiny water droplets, which are the clouds.

## Why does it **rain**?

As the temperature drops, water droplets from the clouds fall to the ground in the form of rain, hail or snow. The water flows into rivers and out to sea, and will later evaporate and fall all over again.

**Did you know?**
Light travels faster than sound. That is why we see lightning before we hear the thunder.

## Why are there **rainbows**?

The white light from the Sun is made up a mixture of the seven colours of the rainbow: red, orange, yellow, green, blue, indigo and violet. We only see these colours when sunlight passes through raindrops, forming a rainbow.

## Why does the **wind** blow?

The Sun does not heat the Earth's surface and the air above it evenly. Where there is warm air, it rises, and cooler air moves in to replace it. This movement of air is what we call wind.

## Why does the Moon change shape?

🌑 The Moon itself does not change shape. It is always round like a ball. One side always faces and is lit by the Sun as it orbits the Earth. What changes is how much of that lit side of the Moon we see from Earth.

**Waxing Crescent**

**1** Only a small part of the lit surface of the Moon is visible from Earth.

**First quarter**

**2** Half of the lit surface of the Moon is visible from Earth.

**Waxing gibbous**

**3** Most of the lit surface is visible.

**Full Moon**

**4** The entire lit surface of the Moon is visible.

## Why do stars come out at night?

🌑 Stars are faraway suns. They shine all the time, but we cannot see them during the day because the Sun, which is the star nearest to us, lights the sky much more brightly.

## Why do we see shooting stars?

🌑 Shooting stars are not real stars, they are meteorites: small pieces of rock in space. As they enter the Earth's atmosphere, which acts like a shield, they are moving so fast that they burn up and glow brightly, just like a star.

## Why is the Sun hot?

🌐 The Sun is an enormous ball of burning gas. The temperature on the surface of the Sun is 5,000 °C and its centre is much hotter. The Sun's extraordinary energy is what heats the Earth and make life possible.

Mercury

Venus

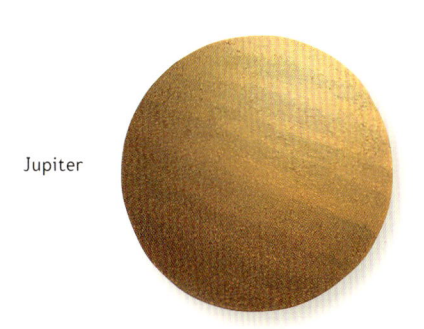

Earth

Mars

Jupiter

## Why isn't there life on other planets?

🌐 The conditions required for life to develop are very complex. As far as we know, no other planet fulfils all the conditions. But there are so many planets in the Universe that we cannot be certain.

Saturn

Uranus

Neptune

Planets of the Solar System

**Did you know?**
The Sun is 110 times bigger than the Earth!

# WHY QUIZZ

Which are the correct answers?

**1** Why don't newborn babies walk?
- **a** Because their brain and muscles still need to develop.
- **b** Because they sleep so much.
- **c** Because they are lazy.

**2** Why do spiders weave webs?
- **a** To look after their babies.
- **b** To trap and eat insects.
- **c** As camouflage to hide in.

**3** Why do zebras have stripes?
- **a** To protect them from mosquitoes.
- **b** For camouflage.
- **c** To make them attractive.

**4** Why are there waves in the sea?
- **a** Because of the Moon.
- **b** Because of the wind.
- **c** Because of all the motor boats and ships.

**5** Why shouldn't we touch mushrooms?
- **a** Because they sting.
- **b** Because they are magic.
- **c** Because some are poisonous.

**6** Why are the tops of mountains white?
- **a** Because it's always cold high up and the snow on them never melts.
- **b** Because that's the colour of the rocks.
- **c** Because they get sprayed with fresh snow from a snow cannon.

**7** Why does the Moon change shape?
- **a** Because the Sun does not light it completely.
- **b** Because we only see part of its lit surface.
- **c** Because a mouse has been eating it.

**8** Why do we have a skeleton?
- **a** It helps us move.
- **b** To dress up at Halloween.
- **c** So we can stand up straight.

**9** Why do dogs wag their tails?
- **a** Because they are happy.
- **b** Because they are excited.
- **c** To keep them cool.

**10** Why are storms noisy?
- **a** Because lightning causes the air to vibrate.
- **b** Because lightning strikes the ground.
- **c** Because the clouds are angry.

**11** Why do boats float on water?
- **a** Because they are lighter than water.
- **b** Because they are lighter than air.
- **c** Because they have fins.

**12** Why do we sleep?
- **a** To rest our body.
- **b** To improve our memory.
- **c** To help us grow.

Answers: 1a 2b 3a 4b 5c 6a 7b 8c 9a 10a 11a 12a b and c!

Other titles in the My First Encyclopedia series:

My First Encylopedia of Dinosaurs

**Text:**
Sophie Lamoureux

**Illustrations:**
Danièle Bour
Laura Bour
Céline Bour-Chollet
Christian Broutin
Ute Fuhr and Raoul Sautai
Henri Galeron
Donald Grant
Héliadore
Gilbert Houbre
Pierre de Hugo
Spopie Kniffke
René Mettler
Daniel Moignot
Sylvaine Peyrols
Jame's Prunier
Pierre-Marie Valat

**Translator:**
Penelope Stanley-Baker

ISBN: 978-1-85-103442-0
© Gallimard Jeunesse 2015
English text © 2016 Moonlight Publihsing Ltd
First published in the United Kingdom in 2015 by Moonlight Publishing,
36 Innovation Drive, Milton Park, Abingdon, Oxon, OX14 4RT
Printed in China